Uncage The Lion Within

NAVIGATE THE JUNGLE OF YOUR MIND TO UNCOVER YOUR PURPOSE, FIND DEEPER LEVELS OF HAPPINESS, AND LET GO OF WHAT NO LONGER SERVES YOU

Zoe Hyde

Zoe Hyde
Uncage the Lion Within
© 2019, Zoe Hyde
Self-published
zoe@zoehyde.com.au

All rights reserved.

No part of this publication may be reproduced, stored in a retrieval system, stored in a database and / or published in any form or by any means, electronic, mechanical, photocopying, recording or otherwise, without the prior written permission of the publisher.

Hardcopy ISBN: 978-0-6485202-0-7
EBOOK ISBN: 978-0-6485202-1-4

Graphics by Inspired By You Designs
Edited by Poly Tzimourtas

For Loren,

Gone too soon, and before you could live out your dream of writing your own book.

This one's for you.

"Maybe being completely free on my own will complete me. Maybe others will follow, or maybe they won't. And maybe one day, I'll be okay with that.

Negativity. Approval. Regret. Doubt.

They can all vanish as I let go and dance in the sunshine of my own self love."

- Loren Failla

"An honest, inspiring and uplifting read of women's lived and learned experiences.

'Uncage the Lion Within' will give you the 'light bulbs', direction, self-reflection and thought-provoking action tasks to enable you to develop a self-loving confidence and …

bring out the lion in you. "

- Trish

"Zoe has taught me to not just focus on the changes I see, but to celebrate the changes I feel."

- Renee

"For years I have always tried to prove to myself and others that I am worthy. 'Uncage the Lion Within' has shown me that I don't need to be some sort of supermum, or to climb Everest to be a success or a hero to my kids; I already am!

Zoe has helped me understand that I can turn failures into learnable moments, habits into goals, negatives into positives, and that I can create a version of myself that I am happy with!

This book truly reflects the meaning of pride in yourself and those around you."

- Sarah

"I have changed from being a 'NO person' to a 'YES person' when it comes to taking opportunities that will challenge me, move me outside my comfort zone, and allow me to take leaps forward in my personal growth and development.

It is so true that if you think within your capabilities, you won't actually stretch yourself. I have been stretched well and truly beyond what I thought were my limits in the past year thanks to Zoe's guidance and support."

- Jeanette

"I've learned that true transformation has to happen from the inside out.

Like most people, I had bit of a scales obsession. I'd only ever do cardio then I'd burn myself out, and binge eat then promise myself I'd start again next Monday. I needed to find a sustainable way to improve the health and emotional wellbeing of both my family and myself.

After experiencing a tough and emotional time in my life, I focused my energy on understanding what triggers my bad habits, what drives me, my core values and what makes me feel good on the inside… (Guess what, it's not chocolate!) Thanks to Zoe's support and assistance, I feel the calmest, happiest and strongest I ever have in my life."

- Kate

UNCAGE THE LION WITHIN

To all the naysayers, the people who doubted my vision, and most importantly, to my inner critic who told me I was not good enough, or worthy enough to succeed:
I am worthy, I am good enough, and I am unstoppable…
And this is just the beginning.

- Zoe Hyde

Contents

1	PRELUDE
3	WHAT STARTED OUT AS A TINY WHISPER, SOON BECAME AN ALMIGHTY ROAR
9	WHO IS YOUR INNER LION?
9	Discover your core values
14	What statement do you wish to make to the world?
17	Action task!
19	"WHY": THE ANSWER TO IT ALL
25	Motivation is not your friend
27	Finding your "why"
36	Action task!
37	ARE YOUR GOALS SETTING YOU UP FOR SUCCESS?
37	Simply place one foot in front of the other
41	The story about the wolf on the hill
43	Short Term Goals
45	Long Term Goals
50	Tying it all together: how to put your goals into action
53	Action task!
54	SUSTAINING THE ENERGY OF YOUR LION

54	Learn to listen to your body
60	Your intuition will guide you; just get out of your own head!
62	Stop allowing your poor health to dull your feelings
74	Instant gratification and our emotional state
79	Action task!

80 WHAT DO YOU TAKE RESPONSIBILITY FOR IN YOUR LIFE?

80	Acceptance or blame?
84	Define your relationship with the controllables
87	Action task!

99 HABITS: DO THEY SUFFOCATE OR EMPOWER YOUR INNER LION?

88	The problem with willpower
90	Understand your habits in order to reframe them
97	Habits: The make or break
100	Reframing our subconscious
104	Careful, the old you will try to come knocking
106	Action task!

107 IT'S TIME TO FIND YOUR PRIDE!

107	The herd mentality
111	How to find a pride who lets you be authentically you
115	How much are you willing to tolerate to either rise up or sit back down?
118	Does your partner want to see you succeed as much as you do?
122	Asking for help isn't a sign of weakness
124	Action task!

125	**OVERCOMING FEARS: THEY DON'T DEFINE YOU**
127	Your comfort zone is the most uncomfortable place to live
130	5, 4, 3, 2, 1 … And just do it!
133	The types of personal fear: Who am I in this?
145	Action task!
146	**LETTING GO AND TAKING BACK YOUR POWER**
146	Lions don't bow as servants to their inner critic
155	Stop comparing yourself to others
158	Past performance programming
162	You're allowed to drink from the spring first, you're a lion for christ sakes!
167	Become your own raving fan
173	Action task!
174	**TAKE ACTION NOW!**
177	Lions speak with integrity
179	Dealing with the inner perfectionist
185	Out with the old, in with the new … rules, that is!
188	Learning to change your state
193	What is your version of happiness? It's time to live it!
196	Action task!
197	**GO FORTH AND ROAR!**
201	**ACKNOWLEDGEMENTS**

UNCAGE THE LION WITHIN

UNCAGE THE LION WITHIN

Prelude

Zoe Hyde owns and operates Zoe Hyde Transformation in a small town of Drouin, in Gippsland, Victoria.

The business has been in operation for almost four years now, and what started as a small home studio, has turned into a 400 square metre facility where women come to exercise, educate themselves on their health, and unleash their potential and happiness.

Zoe works alongside two other coaches: Jeanette Hyde, known formally as Boss Mum, and Erin Tuohy, known as Lil Boss. Together, these girls are focused on changing and improving the lives of women, and having a little (a lot) of fun along the way!

The idea of Zoe Hyde Transformation was born when Zoe was sick and tired of her lack of health, and lack of direction in her life. She always knew she wanted to make an impact on people's lives; she just didn't know to what capacity until she began exercising at a local bootcamp and fell in love with it!

Since that day, her path has been very clear (albeit the occasional bump in the road), and she has remained dedicated to her cause of helping improve happiness, confidence and fulfilment in people's lives.

The book you are about to read was just a pipe dream 12 months ago. Zoe felt stuck in the role of being a personal trainer, but knew she wanted to achieve much more than this. She is firm in her belief that change and happiness starts on the inside, not on the outside, and requires a holistic and healthy approach. This book gives her the capacity to reach the women who feel stuck in diets, body shaming, and a lack of support to feel that they can achieve anything they want in life, including their desired body, if they just look from within!

To Zoe, the lion represents grace, courage, strength and pride: qualities which are greatly admired and respected by her. The lion has an aura about it which exudes leadership and certainty in the most natural and positive way.

To uncage your inner lion isn't to change who you are as a person. No, it's to finally step up and let the authentic you, the one who's been hiding away, shine.

If you'd like to get in touch, you can find Zoe via
www.zoehyde.com.au
Follow Instagram @ zoehyde.author
Join our online Facebook community and group dedicated to personal development, to continue to feed your mind and follow the calling of your own inner lion:
"Uncage the Lion Within"

What started out as a tiny whisper, soon became an almighty roar

Have you ever felt like you have this other version of yourself, waiting to break out of you?

Are you unhappy with the general trajectory of your life, and thought that things would be different for you by now?

I'm here to tell you, you are not alone in this.

Yes, I was burdened by this myself, just five short years ago. However, I can tell you, all we need to do is blink and another year has passed, yet we still battle with feeling stuck in a life we aren't happy with, knowing that we are capable of so much more.

You know, as a teenager and into my early twenties, I used to feel this confident, extroverted person TRYING to break out of me. I knew deep down that authentic Zoe was bold, but I felt captured in this parallel version of myself. I'd completed a degree in a subject I wasn't passionate about, I worked a 9-5 retail job, and I lived for the weekend.

I was stuck in a prison of my own excuses, screaming to escape. To escape from the mediocrity and the lack of clarity in my own life, I just didn't know how. It wasn't until I finally decided to take ACTION and do just something, that slowly but surely the excuses started to wane, and I was able to begin to let the authentic me shine.

I stopped making unfulfilled resolutions, and setting goals I didn't really care about reaching, and just decided one day, that enough was enough.

It's like all those years of shyness, going red-faced if someone asked me a question, and the self-limitation lifted, and the real me could finally stand up and be noticed: to follow my purpose, to live my life passionately and to have the courage to throw myself head-first in to things. When I found this real, authentic me, it's like I could finally breathe, and I had the freedom to live life on my terms.

What first started out as a small, quiet roar of a girl who had discovered her purpose in helping others, slowly grew into a loud, confident and proud roar of a woman who knew what she wanted, and let nothing get in her way of getting there!

My lion was unleashed, and I was determined not to cage her ever again.

Since undergoing my own journey to better health and happiness, I built my own business: a studio and a community where others could feel confident, free from judgement, and encouraged to follow their passions and improve some core areas of their lives: their health, their happiness, and their mindset.

You see, we all rely on external factors to influence how we feel, what we think, and how we should act each day. Think about it, how do you start your day?

Do you go to the toilet then step straight on the scales?

Do you think about a comment someone made to you yesterday which you haven't yet been able to let go of?

Do you wonder if today will be a win or a failure against your own unrealistic expectations of yourself?

We let these external factors define who we are on a daily basis!

If the scales don't give us the answer we were hoping for, we start the day pissed off at our own inability to keep food away from ourselves. If someone said something negative about us the day before, we walk around for the next week playing victim to the story they told us about ourselves, which isn't even true!

Why?

Why do we continue to punish ourselves day in, day out like this?

These things all divide us from one thing: living as our authentic and truest selves!

I speak to many women, of all different backgrounds and circumstances, who insist that weight loss is what will make them truly happy.

But the attachment to the physical representation of you (your body) will not help you get to where you truly want to be. If you are anything like how I used to be, you stand in front of the mirror picking apart your body, thinking about the parts you want to change, and bargaining with the bits you are okay with keeping. Talk about unproductive and soul-sucking!

It wasn't until I stopped focusing on my body changes that I could get out of my own way, and instead put my energy into how I wanted to think and feel!

In order to change any aspect of our life, we must focus on a FEELING, not a LOOK!

Because true happiness and freedom, the kind that lights your soul on fire, is found when we detach ourselves from a physical goal, and embrace the journey of self-discovery we have embarked on.

Deep down, it's easier to blame food or our body shape for why we aren't moving forward in our lives. It gives us a way to keep our true problems at arms length, where we don't have to deal with them. But, whether conscious or subconscious, you know what it is you need to face, you just have to have the confidence to do so.

What health and fitness taught me was that it is a great tool for stress relief, everyday happiness, functionality, and unlocking deeper levels of consciousness in our minds. So many of us coast along, not really aware of how we are thinking or feeling, and not aware of where our bodies sit in space.

When we begin to move more and place a priority on our health, we begin to finally LISTEN to what our body is saying, we begin to FEEL how our posture should be, how good it feels to get our hearts racing, and to listen to niggles or aches we may have. We also become acutely aware of our minds. How we speak to ourselves when we exercise is a pre-cursor to how we speak to ourselves in everyday life: Do you encourage yourself, or talk down to yourself?

Becoming consciously aware of these factors is what helps us begin to improve areas of our lives!

My relationship with health and exercise is an important one; not for the fact of getting abs or a tight, toned body (that doesn't drive me to succeed!), but because by looking after myself, I can function at the capacity I need to in order to fulfil my "why" and my purpose.

It wasn't until I stopped focusing on a look that my path became clear, and I could begin living my "why," which is to help women become leaders, inspirers and role models to the people in their lives, all of who have the confidence to live life on their terms, and go after whatever it is that they want!

And the next step of my fulfilling my "why" was to deliver this book to you: an amazing woman who knows, deep down, that a lion lives inside of her, but she just has to find the key to let it out and let it roar!

So, this book is about overcoming your inner critic, facing your truths, building positive habits, becoming your own raving fan, and most importantly, refusing to live a mediocre, quiet life.

This book is full of action tasks and stories from other women I have the pleasure of knowing, to help you uncover what it is that's holding you back, and how you can get to where you want to go.

Above all else, remain patient on this journey to uncaging your own lion.

It takes time, and sometimes the lessons are right under our noses, but until we are ready to hear them, we won't …

I encourage you to revisit these chapters often, as the more you do, the more you will uncover about yourself and where you are heading!

With that in mind, thank you for going on this wild ride with me!

I hope that my passions, thoughts and ideas help you inject positivity, happiness and confidence into your own life, so that you too, can become the person you were always destined to be!

Who is YOUR inner lion?

If you're like me, I'm sure you've felt the voice of someone deep down inside of you, waiting to escape.

You've been burying it down for a long time, due to fear of the unknown. Occasionally, you hear the words escape you, but you feel so defined by the identity you have given yourself, that you question whether there is hope to ever go after your true calling.

Well, I'm here to tell you that ignoring those calls, and hiding away from your own inner lion is devastating in itself. It's time to start dreaming up a vision of who you really want to be, despite where you currently are ...

I dare you.

DISCOVER YOUR CORE VALUES

Before we jump into things, I want you to think about what your lion represents to you.

What are the core values held highly by your inner lion?

Is she calm, yet powerful?
Strong and driven?
Honest and trusting?

To me, the inner lion isn't ego driven, nor does she have to be overly masculine or dominant.

The inner lion represents the part of you who goes after what she wants, and takes life in her own hands, instead of feeling trapped or defined by her own past or other's limitations.

She holds firm on the values and beliefs which will allow her to live as her best, happiest self.

My inner lion's values are built on trust, honesty, integrity, hard work and connection.

And our behaviours are all driven by our values system.

Connection with others is extremely important to me, and I crave face to face time with people, digging deep into what drives them and who they are as a person. Because I value trust and integrity so highly, I behave in such a way which aligns with this. As soon as someone does something to me or someone around me which goes against my values or moral compass, I have a hard time forgetting that, and I often don't give second chances.

If you're anything like me, you'll have a difficult time trusting those who have done something or behaved in a way which misaligns with your values.

Does this make you a harsh or unforgiving person?

I don't believe so. I think it makes us true to who we really are.

However, what I also have come to understand is I cannot blame someone else for having values that misalign with mine. It's easy to be hurt by another person's actions, and to feel anger and frustration at what they have done. But, if we look closely, perhaps they only did what they did because it was in the interest of THEIR value system!

We need to accept that the person next to us does not share the same values as us, or want the same things as us, so naturally they will behave differently to us. When I learnt this, I could let go of the attachment of emotion I had toward people who had wronged me, and instead remind myself that their values do not align with mine, and that I need to be selective of the time spent with them.

If someone else does or says something which hurts you, yes, by all means protect yourself from that person, but don't buy into it. Simply remind yourself that their values are different, and they may not see a problem with their own actions because what they did was in reflection of their value system. This will save you plenty of heartache down the track!

For one of my clients, Ash, she didn't realise the implication the values of her old workplace had on her until she left and moved elsewhere.

There was a differing of values which conflicted with her own, causing her to feel unhappy.

Her colleagues at her old workplace valued significance and money, and put little value on health, wellness and family time. For Ash, her values were family, happiness and growth, and her new job reflected these values. Her new colleagues stretched her, gave her feedback, praised her when she did well, and valued personal time outside of work. This in turn increased Ash's happiness and confidence, and her mental health improved significantly. Suddenly, she didn't have to feel bad for asking to leave work early so she could get to an appointment, or come to a training session; it was okay for her to work on herself, too.

She understood that the values held by herself and her old workplace didn't align. That didn't make them bad people, they just weren't the right people for Ash to invest her time into because long-term, further conflicts and unhappiness likely would arise.

We will never change what we do or how we behave, until our values change, OR until we change our environment which is causing an inner conflict of values.

But, how can your values help you, you ask?

They help you to narrow down what you believe, the type of person you are, and ultimately, what's important to you. If you understand this, you'll have more clarity when it comes to finding your "why" in the next chapter.

Your inner lion uses her values to help others, to grow, to strengthen herself, and to contribute and enrich other's lives.

What is it that's most important to you in your life?

Does what's important to you NOW align with where you want to go, and the person you want to become?

If your current values system does not align with where you WANT to be, you'll enter a merry-go-round of frustration and confusion when you continuously behave in a way which is counter productive to where you want to be.

For example: You may value security and stability in your life, but you dream of building your own business.

Business, particularly in the first 3-5 years, can be unstable as you build a reputation, find your niche audience, and begin earning profits.

Can you see how these values misalign and could well cause you to take two steps forward, and one step back constantly?

This doesn't at all mean you should give up on your dream, but it does mean that you should question the values your inner lion represents, and begin to attach yourself to values which will help you, not hinder you long term.

A new set of values if you want to start a business may be:

Family: because ultimately, we are in business to give ourselves freedom to spend with our loved ones

Connection: building relationships with prospective clients and employees is extremely rewarding

Achievement: you value making yourself and your family proud

The key here is to jot down every current value you hold, and the values your future self (or your inner lion) want to hold, so you can find out what's working and what's not working for you at this time. (A list of values can be found in your first action task at the end of this chapter)

Remember, the lion does not follow, or seek approval from sheep. The lion builds her own path to success, and protects those she leads.

WHAT STATEMENT DO YOU WISH TO MAKE TO THE WORLD?

The essence of you is not what you do or the label you give yourself, but why you do what you do, and the impact you leave on others.

How do you want to be portrayed in the world?
How do you want to give and help others?
How do you want others to feel when they're around you?

We are all so quick to label ourselves based on something someone has said to us in the past, or a limiting belief we hold on to. But all these labels do is form a habit on how we act, how we feel, and how we treat not only others, but ourselves too!

Why do we continue to hold on to the negative labels we plaster ourselves with, even when we know, deep down, they're false?

I ask of you : What version of yourself do you want to experience life as?

Who do you want to be?
What do you want to do?
If you could BE anything you wanted to be (all limiting factors,
both internal and external aside), what would you be?

Asking these questions of yourself will help to form an understanding of your "why" and your passions in the following chapter.

And once you know these, your inner lion will be a force to

be reckoned with!

For me, I have dreamed of running a successful business, writing a book, being a motivational speaker and coaching people in any area of transformation, and leaving people feeling happier and more fulfilled in themselves. I love being able to turn someone's perceptions of themselves around, helping them become more confident, and seeing them grow into a strong, powerful person!

And I can tell you, I am well on my way to achieving this (well, you are reading my book aren't you?)

However, I was stuck in a set of beliefs that were not only holding me back, but were not allowing me to value my own work or success either. I was stuck between who I WAS, and who I WANTED to be by my belief system, and it was stopping me from finding that essence of myself I was craving.

You see, I believed from personal experience, that to be successful meant to feel resentment and jealousy from those around us, ultimately causing us to be lonely and drive people away.

But, this value system was imprisoning me in my own reality and not allowing me to move forward in my personal and professional life.

I was behaving in a way which aligned with this belief that success equals loneliness. I would keep people at arms' length, downplay my own achievements, and I didn't want to stand out for fear of being perceived as someone who "had it all".

But deep down, I craved connection and building strong relationships with others; and I was so passionate about what I was doing, I wanted to scream it from rooftops.

Because success to me isn't about having the million dollar house, Mercedes Benz and a house maid (although it may be nice)!

Success to me is about helping others, sharing my ideas and my gift, and creating opportunities for others to live the life of their dreams!

If I continued to hold onto my old belief system about success, do you think I would be sitting here, able to call myself an author and a coach?

UNLIKELY!

What I realised was my gifts allowed me to create love, not negativity, to both myself and those around me; I just needed the confidence to realise that the belief I was stuck in was complete and utter bullshit!

Now, take a minute to visualise exactly what it is you want in your life!

Visualise yourself giving to others, putting a smile on your family's face when you walk in the door, helping someone who didn't ask for it, and working on something you are passionate about.

How does that feel?

And, how would it feel to live like this each and every day? (Because it's highly possible!)

ACTION TASK!

Welcome to your first Action Task!

These tasks are positioned throughout the book to help get you thinking and gain an understanding of where you are, and the areas in which you feel you are currently "stuck".

They are designed as a personal reflection of sorts, and I encourage you to work through each one to help you create a personal blueprint to allow you to uncover the authentic you!

Grab a fresh notebook and pen so you can collaborate each action task and refer back to them as need be. You will find that as your awareness and perceptions shift, so do your answers, so I recommend you to work through these questions as often as you see fit.

What values am I currently attaching to? Do they align with where I want to be?

What values do I want to attach to in order to reach my goals and become happier?

What is one small step or decision I need to take now to assist me in going from where I am now, to where I want to be?

An example of some core values:

Success & achievement	Wealth
Personal growth	Fitness
Contributing & giving	Love
Health	Relationships

Community	Fun
Integrity	Authenticity
Comfort	Friendships
Security & stability	Trust
Happiness	Teaching
Freedom	Commitment
Balance	Curiosity
Loyalty	Beauty
Adventure	Fame
Energy	Faith
Creativity	Humor
Inspiration	Leadership
Power	Popularity
Peace	Service
Respect	Wisdom
Career	

"Why": The answer to it all

Where a lot of people fall short is they head into goal after goal, without a real reason for doing so. Without a strong, emotional reason or "why" to change, to chase a promotion, or to complete that five kilometer fun run, any chances of actually achieving your goals diminishes.

Without something to push you, it's easy to give up when you don't feel like it, or to stay in bed on a cold morning, or to tell yourself there's "always tomorrow".

Having a "why", a REAL reason to change will mean you do the work both on the days you feel like it and the days you don't.

But what is a "why"?

It's not the goal.

The goal is the "what", and a lot of people confuse the two.

I have had countless people tell me their "why" is to "get fit and tone up". That's not a "why"; in fact, that's not a really inspiring goal either.

Where a lot of people go wrong is they feel trapped into thinking that "getting fit and toning up" is the main aim of exercising and eating well. But, because this is something they often think they NEED to do, instead of actually WANT to do, any results are short lived. This is why those five words are so uninspiring to me; because they are all too common! It's not until you can sit down and flesh out the reason for actually wanting to prioritise yourself, that you can come up with goals (and a reason for doing so) that are inspiring to you, and something you actually want to achieve!

Your "why" is that thing you've been thinking about for a long time, but have been too scared to be honest about.

It's wanting to feel amazing in your own skin, it's wanting to be a positive role model to your children, and it's fulfilment in doing something you love.

Your "why" can be anything, but it must mean something to you.

It must be that thing that evokes a real emotional response from you when you think about it.

It's important to remember that finding a reason to instil change in your life can be as much about moving away from pain and suffering, as it is about moving towards happiness and pleasure. We just need a strong enough reason to do so, in order to give ourselves leverage and make the "what" a non-negotiable.

Of course, I am of the belief that what we think, we attract, so I feel it's important to focus on what we do want, and not on what we don't. So, if your reason why happens to be about moving away from something painful, then it's important to rephrase it so it becomes something positive we can focus on.

For example, your "why" may be that you don't want to hate what you see in the mirror everyday. By thinking about the fact that you "don't want to hate yourself", you are automatically focusing on the one thing you don't want more of in your life:

hatred!

However, if you can then rephrase this to "I want to love how I look and feel when I look in the mirror each day", you are focusing on bringing more abundance and love into your life.

When you are stuck in negative thinking patterns toward yourself, your body, and who you are as a person, it can become difficult to break that cycle and find a reason to change (and a reason which is strong enough to stop your emotional abuse toward yourself).

But that's okay; this is what we are here for!

If you can't find your real "why" yet, don't panic. It'll come to you eventually, when you are ready to receive it.

Until then, just remember to keep focusing on looking inwards, instead of outwards toward the external and materialistic things that you think will bring you happiness. They won't.

Now, just like our goals can change (and I'll get onto that topic later), our "why" can too.

As you progress through your individual journey, things change.

How you process your thoughts is different, your beliefs and priorities are different, how you see yourself and the world is different, and how you push out of your comfort zone is different too.

When I started my own transformational journey, my "why" was that I wanted to feel confident in my own skin.

I always felt like I was not living up to my true self. I was nervous, shy, didn't know what I wanted, and always compared myself to others. I had a real version of myself in there, waiting to break out, but I just didn't know how to make it happen.

As my confidence grew, so did the real Zoe (and it's hard for most people who meet me now to believe that I was a shy girl, but I was).

I lacked purpose, I lacked direction, and I lacked real happiness.

Along my journey, as I found confidence in myself and my own abilities, my "why" took a shift. As I continued to grow and help others find happiness and health, I was driven less by wanting to "look" a certain way, and more by wanting to be a leader to those around me.

My "why" was driven by the love of helping other people find their authentic selves, too.

What started as a journey to finding confidence in myself became something much deeper, and I feel compelled to help others realise that they are capable of so much more than they give and ask for.

My "why" evolved as I did.

I speak to a lot of women who believe their "why" is to look and feel great on the beach on their family holiday, or at their friend's wedding. I have come to find that most of us aren't driven by a physical "why" and we aren't driven by a particular event or holiday because they come and go.

We all want to feel great for LIFE, not just for a day, so why should our "why" be any different?

I don't believe we can put a tangible time frame on reaching our "why". Not only because it changes and evolves as we do (so we constantly push for more), but also because until we are ready to receive the information and lessons to truly change and begin working on our "why", we won't.

The classic "we only see what we want to see", or "hear what we want to hear", is very true in this case.

As you continue along your journey of discovery, you will slowly begin to take in more information, to truly hear something for the first time (even when you've been told it countless times before), and to begin to receive the lessons which have been waiting for you.

You can't force this process, because it can happen anytime on your journey, most particularly when you have found responsibility in yourself, built great habits, and made some positive shifts to your mindset.

Sometimes it can be years until something "clicks" for us, sometimes months, or sometimes only a matter of weeks.

For me, after building a thriving business, I was left questioning what I was truly working toward. I had brought together a tribe of people who uplifted and supported each other as they improved their lifestyles, but I still didn't have the answer as to what it was all for. I felt burnt out, still not quite fulfilled, and I wasn't sure on the next step to take.

Surprise, surprise, when I tried to force the answer onto myself, it didn't come.

But, when I surrounded myself with people who "got me", who encouraged me to think differently, and who worked in a similar space to me, I received it. Unexpectantly, when I was in the shower (surely I'm not the only one who does her best thinking in the shower? In fact, most of this book was thought up under that waterfall shower head! Great investment I might add!), as soon as I was hit with this reason for "why" I do what I do, everything made perfect sense to me.

Suddenly, I looked at myself differently, as this new spark lit inside of me.

That feeling, the one where you want to cry and laugh at the same time, is the best feeling! That's when you know you are onto something!

MOTIVATION IS NOT YOUR FRIEND

The problem a lot of us face when it comes to getting kick started into the action phase, is we rely too heavily on motivation, instead of being driven by our "why".

Motivation is fleeting. It's like that old friend we all have who only calls us when they need something. It's unpredictable and never sticks around for the long haul!

Your "why", on the other hand, is what helps to create discipline!

I have heard time and time again that what holds people back from achieving their goals is "a lack of motivation". And, if only they found some motivation, they would kick arse and complete absolutely everything they want to!

Man, if I had a dollar for every time I heard this, I would currently be residing on my own island, sipping cocktails.

If you have ever said this, or thought this yourself and you are sick of feeling frustrated by falling in and out of the action phase each time motivation comes and goes, it's time to rethink your approach.

It's time to change your relationship with motivation because it will always be great while it's there, but will cause countless amounts of frustration to you when it isn't.

Perhaps instead of worrying about motivation being the be-all and end-all to the level of success in your life, it's time to think of it instead as a helpful tool we can use occasionally.

You see, motivation is the spark that gets us excited and gets us up and about; but it's discipline that helps us create lasting achievement through forming habits and rituals.

Discipline comes when you want something so badly, that you will do whatever it is you need to do to make it happen.

This is where the relationship between our "why" and discipline is symbiotic.

We can't have one without the other, because it's human nature to only do tasks that make sense to us, and which are ultimately going to help us get to where we want to go.

If you're trying to create discipline to allow you to do something you aren't passionate or excited about, you'll never do it (especially when it's uncomfortable). But, if you create discipline to complete tasks which you understand will help you live out your "why" and your purpose, you'll do it. Whether you feel like it or not, you'll get that shit done because you know your future self, and your inner lion will thank you for it.

The magic comes from getting out of your comfort zone, and getting out of your own way, in order to create discipline to reap the rewards of lasting change!

FINDING YOUR "WHY"

The journey to uncovering your "why" is different for everyone. But we all have the answer, deep down, we just have to find it (and be ready to hear it)!

For some, it can happen when you least expect it, or when you finally look in the mirror and get honest about what you truly want and what you're hiding from. For others, it can be found in your lowest of lows, or in that snap point where you decide that enough is enough.

It takes realising that you are not destined to "settle" to bring about these feelings and questions of "what do I really want?"

I truly believe that everything that happens in our life - the good and the bad, happens to either help us, or teach us.

When you feel like life is kicking you while you're down, it's time to stop asking "why me?", but instead, "what am I NOT seeing or hearing here?"

The universe is an interesting thing, you know.

The more positivity or negativity you project into your life, the more you'll get back in return. You'll be tested, in more ways than you know, and it isn't until you stop playing victim to your circumstances that you will be able to see the lesson that was staring you in the face all along.

All you need to do is stop and take notice.

And the same goes for finding your "why".

Ask yourself:

What am I experiencing in my life, that's trying to point me in the direction of my "why"?

What lesson am I not hearing?

How can I change my default reaction from frustration or anger, to openness, when problems arise?

There are a few different methods you can use to try to understand and find your "why".

Some may work better for you than others, so take some time to trial these and find the best for you.

MIND MAPPING:

One of my favourite methods of finding your "why" is mind mapping. (Yes, I'm a nerd; embrace it!)

I find a mind map encourages you to question everything. Often we will begin with a pretty stock standard answer, but we have to be willing to ask further questions to dig through the soft sand and into the core of the question.

This can happen quite easily, or it can take a few goes.

Quite often when people start coaching with me, I will ask them their "why" and I will get something along the lines of "I want to not hate what I look like in the mirror".

This is the soft sand. Keep digging.

Ask yourself "Why?"

"Why do I hate what I look like in the mirror?"

Because I'm not happy with how my body looks, I have fat thighs.

"WHY": THE ANSWER TO IT ALL

"Why do I think I have fat thighs?"
Growing up my mum told me my legs were too fat.
"How do I think my daughter would feel if I told her that her legs were fat?"

See where this is going?
The "why" is less about how you look, and more about how you feel, or about how you were made to feel.
For the example with this woman, the thought of her own daughter hating her legs, or being told she had "fat legs", is sickening. We all want the best for our families, partners and kids, so we will do anything we need to do to ensure they don't go through similar pain we have experienced.
When you get to the core of this "why", she wanted to be a positive influence to her daughter, to show her that you CAN love your body, despite what others tell you.

When I look at my mind maps, I like to put a big "WHY" in the centre of a page.
Based on this, I will start my own questioning process, with arrows pointing to each answer.
I like to make my mind maps as colourful and pretty as possible.
The more fun you can make it, the better.
This isn't supposed to be a negative process (although you are opening up pain points); it is meant to be empowering and helpful.

For your assistance, I have attached a copy of my mind map. Of course, it started out on paper which I then created on my computer so I could print it and frame it.

THE SUCCESS CIRCLE:

Another way in which you can approach finding your "why" is to instead define what you do want in your life, before assessing your reason for wanting it.

I've come up with this concept called The Success Circle as a way to establish what success means to you in some core areas of your life, instead of as a whole.

Take a look at the circle and define each area by what you would like it to look like in the future, and how you'd like to feel about each.

For example, what does your version of successful friendships mean to you? What do you do together, what type of conversations do you have, and how do your friends make you feel?

Once you have all subcategories defined by what you want (and it's okay if you are happy with where you are now in some

of these areas), ask yourself:
What is this all for?
Why do I want this?

This may help you further establish your "why" when you can look at your desired level of success across all areas.

And even if it doesn't, this can be a great tool to help you define your goals in the following chapter by scoring where you are now versus where you want to be out of 10, and then setting one clear action step for each subcategory in order to help you move forward.

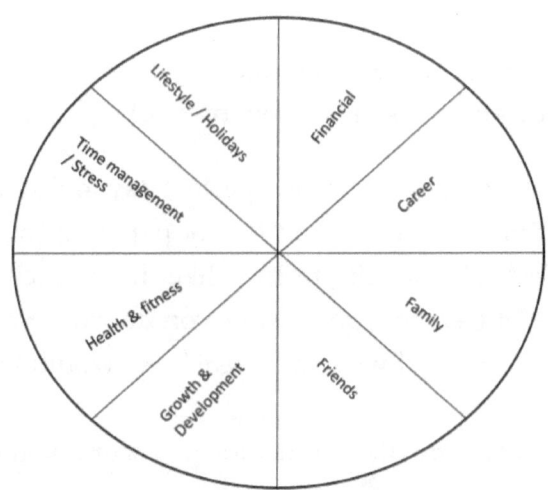

THOUGHT PROVOKING QUESTIONS:

You may like to use this list of probing questions to help you define and clarify your "why". These questions are designed to help you uncover some answers which have been hiding away, in order to move forward and address what it is you truly want, and why.

- What are my top 3-5 core values?
- How do I want people to feel when they are around me?
- Do I follow my head or my heart?
- What does a perfect day look like to me?
- Where do I want to be 1 year from now?
- Where do I want to be 5 years from now?
- What is my version of "success"?
- What is currently not working for me?
- What are my non-negotiables?
- Who is in my inner circle?
- If I don't achieve my goals, what's the worst possible outcome?
- What does my current inner voice say to me?
- Who do I want to inspire or help by working on me?

Going back to defining what a perfect day looks like to you, take some time now to grab a piece of paper and write down what you WANT your life to look like: how much time you spend at the office, the type of work you do, your family, what makes you happy and what an "ideal" day would look like to you.

If your "ideal" day doesn't include any work, you may be in the wrong career.

As humans, we spend over half of our life in the workforce so we gain a sense of fulfilment from what we do. If your work isn't making you excited, challenged or happy, it's time to reassess what will!

When doing this exercise, it's so important to disregard potential barriers like money, time, and any other uncontrollables, and instead focus purely on what it is that you want right now.

ASKING OTHERS:

This is where we can utilise the help of those we hold near and dear to us to tell us who we are to them, what they believe our best qualities are, and what they feel drives us.

We can often be so critical of ourselves that we forgot to see these amazing qualities which make us, US!

Sometimes the people we love know us better than we know ourselves because they have the ability to see the quirks, traits, passions and qualities which we don't see because they are clouded in self-doubt and insecurity.

By understanding how other people view us, we can begin to find confidence in our strengths and talents which are unique to us, and channel them into good.

Find 2-3 of your close friends (those who you know will be completely honest with you) and ask them the following questions:

- How do I make other people feel when they are around me?
- What do you believe are my talents or gifts?
- What can you envision me doing with my life?
- What drives me to work harder each day?
- What do you believe is my strongest core value?
- In what way do you think I could change the world?
- When I'm talking, what topics make me light up?

WHAT DID YOU FANTASISE ABOUT BEING AS A CHILD?

Believe it or not, you may see some correlation between your childhood dreams and your current goals, so looking back at what you "wanted to be when you grew up" could be a great place to start searching for your "why" and purpose.

Before going down the path I am leading now, my vision and goals for my life were extremely unclear.

All I knew was that one day, I wanted to stand up in front of a crowd and be seen; to be known for something. In my younger years this was as an Olympic dressage rider! I used to imagine myself riding in a grand arena, with all eyes on me, breaths held, as I completed my performance.

I realise now that what I really wanted, in a life where I felt invisible, was for people to look at me and feel inspired; to give people hope, courage to chase their own dreams, and a sense of unwavering confidence in their own abilities.

Even though what your teenage-self wanted may not entirely make sense, there could be an underlying message hidden in there, and now is your chance to dig it out!

Now is not the time to think practically. Now is your time to put your worries, fears and angst about money aside and just sit for a moment and THINK!

It's so easy to get caught up in the "buts" and "what ifs" that we stop thinking about ourselves and our own happiness, and instead worry about what others may think of us instead.

We hide behind excuses and fears masked as practical reasoning instead of pushing that shit aside and just being HONEST!

- What did you want to become when you were younger?
- What dreams did you want to chase down?

- Is there any correlation between what you wanted then, and what you want now?
- Can you remember how good it felt to imagine and dream as a child? Go back to that place and soak those positive feelings in!

ACTION TASK!

Take a look back over some of these methods in helping you find your "why".

Have a go at the ones which appeal most to you, and take your time on it. You may not get your answers straight away, but just continue to be honest with yourself, without letting your inner critic, doubt or personal judgement get in your way.

Which method/s worked best for you?
How did it make you feel?
What did you find?
Was it an answer you were surprised by, or something you knew all along?

Pretty up your findings on some nice paper and place it somewhere you can look at it every day. The more often you look at your "why", the more inspired you will become to continue pushing toward achieving it.

Are your goals setting you up for success?

The concept of setting goals is one that is extremely important, yet often misunderstood.

I'm sure you have heard of S.M.A.R.T goals somewhere along the way?
Specific, measurable, attainable, realistic and time bound.

Personally, I find smart goals can feel a little "stuffy", and they don't provide us space to dream up the visions of what we truly want to achieve because they encourage us to place limitations on what we believe is possible at that point in time.

If we were to establish goal which were attainable, realistic AND time bound, we would be placing a glass ceiling over our heads before we could even begin.

At the other end of the spectrum though, we can also be played into the trap that small goals are pointless, which is not the case at all.

Now, I'm not saying that you shouldn't use S.M.A.R.T goals if they work for you, however don't be afraid to create some space for yourself along the way too.

SIMPLY PLACE ONE FOOT IN FRONT OF THE OTHER

So many of us are unrealistic in what we want to achieve in 3, 6, 9 and 12 months, yet we struggle to look further forward to the next 2, 5, 10 or 20 YEARS!

We put these ridiculous expectations on ourselves every time a new year rolls around, then shortly after, beat ourselves up for not being able to "stick with it".

Why?

Because we overcomplicate the process.

We think what we want will magically appear in the absence of hard work and commitment. And we believe that if we throw enough arrows, eventually one will hit the target.

But continuing to set goals that don't light your soul on fire is completely and utterly pointless.

Often we set a goal of weight loss, or to run ten kilometres, because people around us are doing it, so we should too!

It's time to stop conforming to society and set realistic goals which allow you to slowly but surely chip away at things so you can fulfil your "why" and your purpose!

Sounds too simple, right?
But it's true!

We continue to be frustrated at ourselves each year for failing our attempts at yet another boring and unfulfilling goal, in the hopes that we will feel "successful" if only we achieve them.

I'm here to tell you guys: It's time to step up and assess your goals very carefully.

Stop with the broad, boring goals of "getting fit" or "making more money", because it doesn't work, and yes, you will likely fail.

Where is the purpose?

It's time to start with your "why" then work your way to slowly breaking down what steps you need to take in order to fulfil your "why". Because at the end of the day, living your purpose will bring you the ultimate sense of achievement.

And yes, it's very normal for our "why" to evolve and change, and that is okay. Just make sure you reassess your goals and make modifications to them as need be.

An important rule of thumb is that your goals are merely stepping stones. Each goal has a purpose, which is to take you one step closer to your "why" each time.

They should be well thought out, strategic, realistic, and most importantly, push you a little bit harder each time.

I know, I know! As a high achiever this is something I struggle with myself because I want everything done and ticked off NOW. But I know this will lead to frustration and unproductive activity later.

Hell, it wasn't until I actually broke down exactly each point I wanted to make in THIS book that I started to make progress. Before then I was flailing about, concerned about my word count on a book that had a title and some rough chapter ideas, but not much else.

It freaked me out! Each week I would say "Okay, I'm going to write a thousand words today". But without direction and purpose, I wrote well, but it wasn't cohesive, and it wasn't helping me achieve my target: which was to finish it!

Since breaking things down, implementing a solid plan and keeping myself accountable, I have been able to take productive action which propelled me forward to finishing this, all with the purpose of one thing: to help more people find happiness, feel more in control of their own lives, and become positive leaders to those around them.

Your goals don't have to be complicated or fancy; they just need to have meaning. When we attach them to our "why", they become easier to work on because we have a clear reason for doing them. But, understand the importance of writing these goals down. It is not enough to keep your visions and dreams in your head. By writing them down, they become tangible and can be carried into our conscious thought, where they are more likely to occur.

And if you aren't quite clear on your "why" yet, that is absolutely okay!

Simply set some goals based on where you think you want to go NOW, because you can always reassess and come back to things later!

THE STORY ABOUT THE WOLF ON THE HILL

Have you ever heard the story about how the wolf on the hill is always hungrier than the wolf who's already at the top of the hill?

And while I write these words I realise this is a book about unleashing your inner lion, but let's roll with the wolf for now.

If we are constantly seeking the end destination, we have already lost, because we will never be hungry for any more. The same relates when we believe that we no longer need to learn, or grow, or achieve anything more. Complacency sets in, and for you, who's reading this book to escape the mediocre, complacency is not a nice place to live.

If you haven't already realised, this is about so much more than reaching your goals. It's about growing into the person you NEED to become in order to live your "why", your purpose.

Once we outgrow a hill and reach the top, it's time to find a new hill. A bigger, more challenging hill. This will push you to take risks, set bigger goals, and strive for more in all aspects of your life. The top of the hill is where ego and complacency breeds, so don't stay there too long.

When you reach the top, ask yourself a simple question: "Am I honestly where I want to be yet?"

Now, I'm not to say that you shouldn't look for happiness and pride in making it to the top of your hill; you most definitely should! I'm just simply reminding you not to settle.

Look at these hills as your small, short to medium term goals which serve as stepping stones to your "why" and where you envision your life!

This is where short term mindsets serve us well. They allow us to break down the big, scary Everest looming over us into manageable sized mountains. And on every hill and mountain, we learn, we experience, and we find the lessons that we need in order to tackle the next one.

SHORT TERM GOALS

What are short term goals, you ask?

As I've just mentioned, they are simply a way to set smaller, shorter time-framed goals which will lead into the next goal, and the next one, until you begin to get closer to your "why"!

Put simply, they are your big long term goals, broken down into more manageable chunks!

But they have to be realistic. We can't rush the process of success and greatness. There are many hurdles to jump first, and unfortunately the "quick fix" mentality which is bred into us these days, doesn't help.

I talk to women who have battled with their weight for 20+ years, who expect it'll only take 12 weeks to correct their metabolism and get to their goal size.

Nothing could be further from the truth!

We must be willing to play the long game. To learn, to fall down and pick ourselves up again, to grow, and to slowly tick things off our lists.

Success happens in the journey to reaching your "why". Without the hardships, the struggles and the helping hand along the way, we wouldn't become the resilient lion we need to be.

When thinking of your small, short term goals, don't try to make them bigger and better.

Remember the K.I.S.S principle?

KEEP IT SIMPLE, STUPID!

Stop overcomplicating things.

These goals should be action tasks you need to perform daily, weekly, or monthly to help you reach your bigger, longer term goals.

These could be things like :

Walk for 20 minutes every day
Make that phone call you've been putting off
To put down 300 words into your book
To set up your office so it is a cohesive, workable space you enjoy being in

Make sense?

Even if the goals sound ridiculously small, they serve a purpose in building your confidence to "get shit done", to make you feel a sense of achievement, and to help set you up for success later! So, in these circumstances, leave no stone unturned!

If you feel some small task will help you later on, do it, and then celebrate achieving it!

LONG TERM GOALS

Now, onto the long term goals and mindsets!

These are the goals you want to complete in 1, 2, 3, 5 and so on, years!

Now, the relationship between our long and short term goals is VERY important; more so than you realise. Just like we breed complacency at the top of the hill, we can breed it at the bottom, when we believe we "have plenty of time" to achieve our goals!

I've seen it play out before, trust me!

When we have long timeframes attached to things, and even when we are realistic about how long it is going to take to achieve these big goals and fulfil our "why", we can set ourselves up for laziness IF we are not accountable and consistent to our short terms goals.

Let's say for example, you want to start up your own business. Awesome, right?

You know what services you want to offer, you know what you want your branding to look like. You understand the customers you want to attract.

BUT, you know it's going to take 2 years to be in a financial position to be able to begin AND you need to be at home with your young kids.

Imagine how easy it is to say "I don't need to do any market research this month, because I'm years away from starting anyway!" We can very quickly trap ourselves into believing that time will work in our favour, and that we don't have to start YET if we are a while off taking action.

This is exactly where I have seen people come unstuck!

They may have a great "why", it may drive them emotionally, and they may really, really want to achieve success. But if they have no correlation between their short and long term goals, they can easily take their foot off the gas and "try again tomorrow".

But tomorrow never comes, right?

What we need to do is to understand the relationship between all our goals and our "why".
Start at your "why":
"What is it that I truly want and how do I want to feel, contribute and achieve?"
Then, ask yourself:

"What do I need to achieve long term to do this?"
There may be just one thing, or there could be four or five things. That's okay.
Now:
"How can I break up these big goals into manageable, bite-sized chunks?"

Allow me to give you an example of how I have done this within my own business and transformation studio.

My "why" is to build leaders and role models who know what they want, and are not afraid to go after it. These women view their health and their bodies as a vehicle to their success, happiness and sense of adventure.

Now how the hell do I achieve this, you ask?
Don't worry, I asked myself the same thing when I started!

Some of my long term goals which help me fulfil this "why" go like this:
- To build a thriving community of 100 like-minded women who all support and encourage one another.
- To become a personal coach which will enable me to help women one on one in breaking down any barriers, and defining what it is they truly want.
- To speak around Australia to groups of women all seeking to break free of the mediocre, but who are currently feeling "stuck" in their circumstances and mindsets.

So to break these down into smaller goals, I did the following:

Goal 1: Build a community of 100 women.
- Extend our current facility to allow us to help more women.
- Educate and mentor our new trainer so I can empower her to lead others too.
- Raise awareness of what we do in our local community through running events and seminars which help women feel empowered and educated.
- Give advice and support to women online and face to face to help them enter the "action phase".

Now this was just for my goal of building a larger community, but do you see what I did there?

When I have these sub-goals down on paper, I can then break it down to what I need to do in order to get there.

I implemented tasks like planning and hiring trades to complete an extension of our studio, helping my new trainer break down what's holding her back so she can feel confident in her own abilities and fulfilled by the work of helping others succeed, and setting dates in my calendar for events and workshops and marketing them to the local community.

Completing these smaller tasks or goals allowed me to take further steps toward my bigger goals.

Another problem which you may face when it comes to your goals is what happens when you feel you aren't making the appropriate amount of progress to propel yourself to where you want to be.

I have seen this play out before, and would love to share a story of a beautiful woman I have the pleasure of working with.

Kate had set some huge goals for herself, and had a strong, emotional reason for achieving them. However, after a rollercoaster of a year juggling a chronically ill child, taking care of her family, working full time and managing a team, and committing to her training and new lifestyle, she was struggling with the goals and progress she had not quite been able to reach.

A pattern I noticed emerging for Kate was that anytime a barrier came up, or things didn't quite go to plan, she would make her goals SMALLER as a way to still feel that sense of achievement in completing something.

But what implication did this have over her long term goals?

She would cut herself off at the knees, and before giving herself a chance to TRY to accomplish a goal, she would write it off as "too big" based on her progress thus far.

What was most important to her, and what would bring her happiness, love and health, was fading further and further away, and the excuses as to why she wouldn't get there would begin to appear.

In Kate's own words, she realised that while making her goals smaller in order to feel a sense of achievement was giving her some level of instant satisfaction, they were not contributing to her long term sense of happiness and fulfilment, as she was "giving herself more rope to hang herself with".

Something to learn from Kate's story here is that "life happening" is inevitable. There will always be roadblocks, struggles, and sacrifices which need to be made.

But, we cannot give up what we truly want based on if we fall down or face temporary problems.

What matters is you get up that 1 time out of 100 and keep going!

Kate learnt many valuable lessons in her hardest year, all of which shaped her mentally into the woman she needed to become in order to achieve her biggest goals!

TYING IT ALL TOGETHER: HOW TO PUT YOUR GOALS INTO ACTION

Now that you are clear on exactly what it is that you need to do, and why you need to do it, we need to direct our attention to the glue that holds it all together: accountability!

When we find the relationship between our goals and our "why" or purpose, it becomes a lot easier to begin to take those positive steps forward.

However, sometimes this just isn't enough!

A vast majority of the population readily manage the expectations of others, but find it hard to meet their own needs.

Why?

Because they are what I call the "Yes women"!

They say "Yes" to others, often before they have even had time to think about it and what it would mean to them. Saying "Yes" is a habit!

And, often to the frustration and annoyance of themselves, they still do it!

Without accountability, who will help us on those days we can't be bothered, or when it's cold, or when we want to give up?

If you are anything like me, your word is your bond. And if you tell someone you are going to do something, you bloody well do it!

The question is, how do we use this to our own advantage when it comes to getting shit done for ourselves?

ARE YOUR GOALS SETTING YOU UP FOR SUCCESS?

We rely on external accountability!

We have someone there we need to answer to, who we know will ask us the hard questions as to if we have completed X task to help us get to our goal!

Your accountability "person" needs no agenda of their own if they take on this role. They simply need to care for us, and want to see us succeed!

This person can't be the one who will make excuses for us not getting our shit done!

They can't tell us "It's okay, you're busy, take a few days off."

NO!

They need to watch over us, be there to hold the mirror up to ourselves when we start bullshitting why we didn't achieve our tasks, and they need to grab our hand and pull us back up again, and set the eye on the target!

Do you have someone in mind yet?

I want you to find someone who cares for your success so deeply, that they'll be honest to you when you need it!

It's your job to tell this person what you're going to do, and when, and report back to them with what you did!

If you struggle to put yourself and your wishes first, it's time to look at your action tasks as appointments to yourself.

Your dreams and goals are important to you, aren't they?

You wouldn't cancel an appointment for a loved one if it meant they would become healthier and happier, would you?

So why do we constantly do it to ourselves?

I'm not saying you have to say "screw it" to your loved ones, and their needs.

Or your co-worker who keeps dumping their work load onto you (but then in fact, maybe you do).

I'm just saying that each day, you put time aside for YOU too!

Because the result of not doing so will cause you endless frustration with yourself that everyone else around you is happy and feeling cared for, but YOU. It'll be like their life is going by, and you are stuck being the passenger to your own life, with your goals, dreams and desires slipping through your fingers as if you are driving past your turn-off at 100 km an hour.

Do you want that for yourself?
Didn't think so.
And the fact you are still reading this book proves that.

When we, the women who struggle with staying accountable to our own needs, can flip things on their head and create some level of external accountability tied to our own tasks, we'll be productive, we'll take steps forward, and the frustration will cease.

Who is your person who can help you stay accountable to yourself?

ACTION TASK!

Take some time to record both your short and long term goals.

Do they align with where you want to go? Will achieving them help you toward fulfilling your why?

Ask yourself, what is the likely outcome if you DON'T achieve your goals, and let yet another year of inaction occur?
What does your life look like? Are you happy?

Who can you ask to help you stay accountable?

What is one small thing you can do NOW which will help you get started?

Sustaining the energy of your lion

In order to create lasting change in any area of our lives, we need to ensure what we are doing is maintainable, and part of a new normal for us. If we want to channel the greatness of our inner lion, we need to avoid burn out, avoid quick fixes, and become acutely aware of our bodies, how we feel, and rest accordingly.

LEARN TO LISTEN TO YOUR BODY

Something we tend to lose as we age, become busy, and start "adulting" is the ability to listen to our own bodies.

These natural in-built behaviours we are born with are thrown out the window when "life" gets in the way.

Think about it: as a child, you would cry when you were hungry, tired, sick or injured. All you had to worry about was how YOU felt! You would eat when you were hungry, and stop when you were full. You would sleep when you were tired, and wake when you were rested.

But, as soon as we become busy, go off to work, and look after our families, we begin to neglect ourselves very quickly!

When was the last time you took twenty minutes for yourself on the couch when you were run down?

I'd take it you didn't, and instead you pushed through,

putting everything (and everyone) else ahead of your own needs!

Our bodies aren't stupid. In fact, they are acutely smart, and often when they are telling us something, it's for a reason. We just need to stop and listen.

But we don't!

We run from one thing to the other, without much concern for ourselves, only on getting through our to do lists, chores and jobs before going to bed and doing it all again tomorrow.

If you want to let you inner lion shine, it's time to listen. We all have one mouth and two ears for a reason, you know!

You see, this is an important lesson I had to learn from myself. As a high achiever, and someone who strives to succeed day in-day out (particularly in a business I am extremely passionate about), I had to learn the hard way when it was okay to slow down (yes, believe it or not, it is okay), and when I could push that little bit harder.

Every few months for a couple of years, I would suffer burnout. The kind that had me sick for weeks on end, or in bed, unable to eat because the constant stress to my body from being in fight or flight for extended periods slowed my digestion and other normal functions.

I didn't get enough sleep, I was burning the candle at both ends because I wanted everything to be "done right now", and as a result, I didn't take care of ME.

But without me, I didn't have the success, the work or the achievement.

Can you relate?

It was time for me to get REAL with myself!

I had to remind myself that there is always tomorrow. If I don't finish things today because I needed to have some down time or rest my eyes, it's okay!

If I'm being honest, that thought used to scare the living daylights out of me!

I used to think I would DIE if I didn't get my work done for the day.

I had to realise that in order to feel happy and fulfilled, I couldn't keep up with what I was doing to myself, because that in itself was making me miserable.

I was a leader of health and fitness, but I wasn't walking my talk. In fact, I was constantly running on empty.

In order to break the cycle of self-neglect, I had to first understand the implications of what I was doing in relation to my family, my business, and myself.

- Did I want to be sick all the time?
- Did I want to be moody and emotional because I was exhausted?
- Did I want my relationship to suffer because I couldn't give my best self to my partner?
- Did I want my clients to follow in my footsteps and burn themselves out too?

Nope!

Sometimes we have to take ourselves to these points of pain, and these worst case scenarios in our minds, to really understand what our current behaviours are doing to us.

I grew to understand that looking after myself would actually make me MORE successful because if I felt rested, energised and less stressed, I would in turn become more productive each day!

Sure, now I may take an hour or so off some afternoons to watch trashy TV and free up my mind before my evening work, but the work I completed before then was at a higher standard, and had a bigger impact on the overall running of my business.

When I realised how my actions were having such a negative experience on myself and those around me, I became more aware of how I was feeling, how I was thinking (was I catastrophising due to stress, or maintaining a level head?), and what I needed in order to bring out my best self.

I had to ditch the mentality of needing to be superhuman, and instead focus on just being the best human I could be.

So, now I prioritise rest. I say "No" to evenings out if I feel a night on the couch will be best for me in the long run, I sleep well, I check myself constantly if I begin to feel stressed, and I know when to push for that little bit more, and when to back off.

The overall result?

- I'm happier.
- I'm healthier.
- I no longer hold on to little comments in my head and replay them for hours on end.
- I don't get sick often at all, whereas before it was every month to two months.
- I'm more focused.

- I feel like I am taking leaps forward to my "why", whereas before I felt like I was stuck, furiously paddling but making no progress.

Wouldn't you love to do the same?

Have a think about what your body is trying to tell you when burnout is approaching?

Are there patterns which form each time you are over-worked or over-stressed?

We can't break the cycle until we stop and listen to what our body is saying, and why.

It may be that you break out in a rash when you are stressed, or you gain a persistent headache, or you crave foods you normally wouldn't think twice about.

Our body is sending us clues constantly, and when we can learn how to read them, we can actively prioritise our rest and recovery before the situation worsens.

Now, I'm not saying you have to have a week long vacay (although it would be nice!).

You could adopt any form of self care, so long as it helps you refocus and recover.

This could be something like taking 20 minutes for a hot bath, indulging in your favourite TV show, asking your partner to put the kids to bed so you can have some time alone to get creative, or taking the morning off work to sleep in.

These don't have to take up big chunks of time, they just have to be effective in helping remove some chaos and allow some space to breath.

SUSTAINING THE ENERGY OF YOUR LION

If you can take small amounts of time for you now (when you need it), you can prevent causing complete burn out for yourself, which could well result in a whole week spent on the couch or in bed instead. Because if you continue down your current patterns of burnout, just like I had, your inner lion will become muffled, and her roar weakened.

YOUR INTUITION WILL GUIDE YOU, JUST GET OUT OF YOUR OWN HEAD!

We all know about those "gut feelings" we get, right?
But how often do you actually follow them?

For a lot of us, we ignore what our gut is telling us and instead follow what our mind tells us, only to later realise we've been led down the wrong path. When we follow our head, we doubt, we overthink and we ignore any alarm bells and simply do what we "think" we need or want at that time.

Do you ever use a pros versus cons list when you have a difficult decision to make? Even when, deep down you know what you need to do?

Yep, we are all guilty of it.

We are susceptible to ignoring what FEELS right over what makes sense, even if all signs point to following our feelings.

Often we wait until we have had the lessons, and repeated the mistakes, until we finally decide to listen to the senses of our gut and our heart. Learn to trust what it is telling you, because more often than not, your intuition is right.

It's time to stop ignoring the inner dialogue deep in your heart and in your gut, and start listening to where it is guiding you instead. We all want to do what's logical, but logical doesn't always mean better, or help us long term.

My experience with my intuition has been a positive and empowering one. Often, I'll be talking to someone, or coaching them through a problem, and I am guided into this incredible knowledge which I can use to help them move forward. I have no concept of where it came from, or how I knew the information; I just find it when I need it the most.

And that, my friends, is truly magical!

A true lioness will follow her intuition or gut feeling, and be totally in tune with what it is telling her. Our intuition is the centre for our wisdom and if we allow ourselves to trust it, we will be led on an incredible journey, all the while feeling fulfilled as we walk in alignment with our values.

STOP ALLOWING YOUR POOR HEALTH TO DULL YOUR FEELINGS!

One of the most important pieces of the puzzle is our health. In order to achieve great levels of success, happiness and fulfilment, we must look after ourselves!

Not doing so dulls our ability to LISTEN to what we are feeling, thinking, seeing and doing.

Our health is the centre to our mindset and intuition. And my inner lion was only uncaged when I began to prioritise my health and take care of ME! Before then, the voice of my authentic self, of my inner lion was unable to be heard!

Where in your life do you value and prioritise the following?

- Sleep
- Managing stress
- Nutrition
- Movement

And, which of these areas in your life needs improvement?

As I said earlier on, it's not about weight loss being the front and centre of WHY you should value your health. But, if you can improve these aspects of your life, not only will you function and perform better each day, but your physique will naturally become a by-product of the positive, daily habits you insert into your life.

If sleep is a problem for you, what does your nightly routine look like? Are you switching off from work mode, or do you lay awake for hours with your mind running laps?

Are you consuming too much sugar and caffeine close to bed time and unable to get to sleep? Are you staying up late watching mindless shit then wake exhausted each day?

Whether you realise it or not, each of the factors of health I have mentioned impact each other on a daily basis!

If you are stressed, you sleep poorly, you make poor eating choices, and as a result of this you are too tired or run down, or feel too horrible to move your body.

It's all inter-connected.

And it's not about becoming perfect, it's about making small improvements to these areas which can dramatically shift how you feel.

Do this, and you will start to think, feel and behave at a higher level. Your inner lion will be heard, and will guide you to where you want to go!

What are some small shifts you can begin making in your life right now?

SLEEP:

To put it simply, your bed should be for sleep and sex. That's it!

When we begin to watch TV in bed late at night, or lay awake in the dark with our minds churning, we disrupt our sleep patterns which will in turn wreck havoc on our performance the following day.

If you are someone who lays awake for hours thinking, get up!

Make a hot drink and journal your thoughts and ideas onto paper. Our minds have a way of catastrophising, and playing things over and over so often, that we begin to shift the story we tell ourselves about what we experienced.

By writing down what's in your head, you'll find it's never as bad as it originally seemed.

I find I need to do this with my own to-do lists. If I keep it in my head and play over and over what I need to do for the day, I stress myself out and feel overwhelmed by the enormity of the task. But, if I take five minutes to sit down and write down exactly what I need to do, I find 99% of the time, it's not actually as bad as I thought.

We need to stop giving in to what our minds are telling us, and instead find the truth by writing it onto paper and analysing what we were so worried about in the first place.

If you struggle to switch off from work, it's time to STOP checking emails late at night. Disable your work email from your phone, so you have to actually get up to the computer to sneak a peek of what's happening at the office.

The same applies if you own and operate a business. Clients expect you aren't going to respond at 11pm, however they will email or message you at this time because they've thought of something or want to ask a question. That's okay, however, we must set the expectation that at a certain time of day, we will not respond. Your clients or customers will understand, and you won't lose them because of it, trust me!

We are human after all, and we need to wind down and switch off too!

What are you eating prior to bed time?

Is it calorie laden and full of processed sugars and poor quality fats? This in itself will cause disturbed sleep as your body tries to metabolise the sugars. Instead, try a cup of herbal tea, or if you do need to eat close to bed (which is totally fine), just ensure you are including a source of protein too.

Opt for something like yoghurt and fruit, chia seed puddings, or a small smoothie!

Set yourself a reasonable bed time which works for you and where you feel you can function well during that next day. Sleep is different for everyone, but get too little, and you will feel foggy and unclear! For myself, I sit comfortably around the 6.5-7 hours mid week, however by Friday, I begin to sleep that little bit more after a long and busy week.

Find what works for you, but I'm sure we could all benefit from an extra fifteen to thirty minutes each night!

STRESS:

As I have just mentioned, our minds have a knack of catastrophising things for us and making them seem worse than they appear.

Small amounts of "stress" can increase productivity and performance. If you're anything like me, I work well to timeframes and feeling "rushed", so I will do a lot of work when I know I only have an hour before I need to leave the house!

However, long term stress will not aid us in any way! When

we are in these states of high stress, it can become harder and harder to help ourselves and we will constantly push our own health and wellbeing to the wayside!

You see, I have no trouble switching off after completing small short bursts of work under a "stressful" environment. But, put me in a state of stress and busy-ness for an extended period of time, and I will fall to mush!
We all would!

Not only does constant stress affect how well we complete our work, it also increases our cortisol and puts us in a state of fight or flight mode. The implications of this on our health long term are drastic, and blood is pumped away from our digestive organs and to our extremities ('cause back in the day, cavemen had to outrun their opponents and they couldn't do that while thinking of food)!
So, what happens when we remain in "fight or flight" mode? Our digestion slows, our metabolism slows (long term), and we begin to fuel ourselves poorly because we are either not hungry, or have cravings for high energy, sugar and caffeine laden foods.

When we are in a state of constant stress, it's like we are living in a fog! We can't think clearly, our decision-making abilities are impaired, and it becomes harder to see the road ahead!
It's hard to pull yourself out of this state if you have been living that way for a long time, but when you do, you will realise just what you were missing out on!

What can you do to reduce the stress in your life?

- Learn to switch off from work when you are home!

Set rules for yourself that you MUST follow: these could be things like allocating a time to put your phone down at night, scheduling "game night" with the family, or ensuring you read a good book for 15 minutes each night.

For me, I initially struggled with this concept but the longer I held true to my new set of rules, the easier it became, and the quicker I could switch off. Trust me, your family will thank you for it!

- Move, often!

I can't even begin to tell you how important exercise is for your overall happiness and mental health! In a state of stress, often the last thing we want to do is get up and move, but force yourself to! You will clear your mind and get an incredible rush of endorphins (more so than when you eat chocolate)!

You don't have to do hours of exercise each day. If you are time poor, commit to just 10-20 minutes at a time, or go for a leisurely stroll. Once you feel you can handle more, increase the amount and type of exercise you do. For example, what may have once been a simple walk could turn into a group fitness session at a local training studio

- Do something you enjoy!

We all have a hobby or some activity we love. What's yours? Have you been pushing it to the wayside because you've been "too busy"?

It's time to prioritise some time to it each day, or every couple of days!

You don't have to dedicate hours if you don't have hours. Even just 10-15 minutes spent doing something you enjoy can be enough to put you in a great state of mind!

Whether it's cooking, reading a book, sitting and playing with your kids or fur babies, watching your favourite trashy TV show, photography, or jigsaw puzzles (please tell me I'm not the only one who loves puzzles)! Whatever it may be for you, do it!

- Break the pattern of stress!

As soon as you notice a state of stress or overwhelm come over you, the best thing you can do is break your current state!

If you are sitting down, progressively becoming more worried, get up and MOVE for few minutes!

Bust some tunes and have a boogie, do 20 star jumps on the spot, walk a lap of the office, or step outside and breathe some fresh air!

Just break your current state! Staying in it will not help you; you have to break free.

I found for me, once I learnt this concept of changing my state, my life changed dramatically, and for the better!

I no longer feel bogged down in my own thoughts as I feel them dampen my mood and worry me in states of stress. Instead, I am consciously aware of what I am saying to myself and how I am feeling, and as soon as I feel myself lose control to stress, I get up and move.

I don't care how stupid you think you'll look, try it!

Get some Beyonce blaring and stand up and boogie!

NUTRITION:

You've probably heard the saying: Your car won't run on dirty fuel, so your body shouldn't either.

The food we choose to put in our bodies can either fuel us for success or for defeat. We can end up living in one vicious cycle unless we can take the time to break the pattern and learn and understand why and how we can fuel ourselves better!

When we are tired or stressed, we use sugar and high energy "foods" to give us that hit of energy we need. Yet half an hour later we are still hungry and have just suffered from yet ANOTHER sugar crash, so we go and buy ourselves another can of coke or chocolate bar!

And so the cycle begins!

What if I told you that you could create sustained energy levels throughout the day by simply improving your food choices?

No sugar rushes or sugar crashes, and no 3pm munchies. Every day you have the power to feel charged up and ready to go!

If it sounds too good to be true, I can assure you it isn't, because it is highly possible to achieve this and still have balance and enjoyment in your life!

All food choices are emotional, and food is used to celebrate any and every occasion. I'll be the first to admit I LOVE food!

What do I do? I enjoy all the things I love, but in moderation. I find enjoyment from trialling new flavours and seeing how I can jazz up my veggies to make them exciting to eat! And when I do this, my cravings subside, and the treats I do have give me a higher level of satisfaction in a smaller quantity. Win!

I can assure you it isn't as hard as it sounds. When you are fuelling your body with good quality nutrients, you will feel better, you will think clearer, you will have more energy, and as a result, you will be more productive and happier! And you will begin to crave feeling this good ALL the time, so you will consciously make the effort to keep your body full of "clean" fuel!

The first step to making positive improvements to your food intake is to REPLACE it, not cut it!

Every diet out there encourages us to reduce our food intake, but this in turn leads to bingeing episodes when we feel tired, stressed or upset. So, instead of cutting your intake, replace it:

Eat plenty of colourful fruits and vegetables that you enjoy, high quality grains, omega 3 fats and proteins. Reduce the amount of packaged foods in your day and experiment with new flavours and food combinations.

And of course, stop with the food rules!

Yes, every diet you have ever followed probably had a different set of rules or guidelines to follow.

"You can't eat white foods", "Carbs are the devil", "Coconut oil is king" ... See where I'm going with this?

We have heard so many rules in our lives when it comes to food that we've forgotten how to stop and listen to what our body is asking for instead!

I encourage you to take things back to basics with the suggestions I've made and find foods you like to eat, that still contain nutritional benefits. No, you don't need to eat boiled chicken and rice every day!

Last but not least, something that too often we forget when it comes to food is what we are drinking!

What tends to happen when we begin a process of improving our nutritional intake is we forget to look at what we are drinking too.

Soft drinks, wine, iced coffee … I could go on!

These drinks we choose to consume each day are hidden energy bombs.

So the same should go for our drink choices: REPLACE, don't cut!

Opt for water first and foremost as we all know we could be making significant improvements there. Then choose options with a lower sugar intake such as tea, black coffee, soda water and lime, and homemade ice tea, then watch your energy levels transform!

MOVEMENT:

We often forget the role that exercise can play on our mental health, reduction in stress, and overall happiness!

Sure, some days I also suffer from a good 'ol case of the CBF's! But, I always remember how I know I will feel after moving my body; and it's always positive.

Exercise can make us feel accomplished, confident, and mentally stronger; and these are all things we could do with more of. You don't have to commit to hours of training each and every day because you simply don't have time for that!

Instead, adopt the quality over quantity approach.

Which do you believe is more effective?

1. Walking/dawdling on the treadmill watching trashy TV for an hour?
2. 15 minutes of high intensity bursts on the treadmill at 30 seconds as fast as you can, and 30 seconds rest?

More does not always equal better, so I hope you picked option 2!

It's no wonder we never commit to moving more when we are already stretched for time and believe we have to commit an hour or more each time we do!

My philosophy is always start small and work up from there.

As much as you want to go from zero to hero, this mentality probably hasn't served you well in the past. Instead, make it manageable. Start with moving for 3 days a week somewhere in the vicinity of 10-30 minutes, then slowly but surely build up to 4 days a week, then 5.

Any movement is positive movement to get started, so if you aren't ready to tackle the higher intensity options, start with a walk, or a bike ride!

The stronger and fitter you begin to feel, the more you will want to move, which will be a fantastic stress reliever, and a confidence and happiness booster!

You will notice that when you can begin to improve each of these 4 important areas of your health, you will start to unleash the authentic version of yourself who has been in hiding, dulled by the stress, the sugar, and the lack of energy! Shifting your focus from how you look, to how you feel, will help you understand that our happiness, our performance, and our potential, are driven from our internal bodies.

Aim for small, 2% improvements in these areas each week and celebrate every achievement along the way.

INSTANT GRATIFICATION AND OUR EMOTIONAL STATE

Our emotional state and the expectations we place on ourselves can have a lot to do with how we implement some healthier routines in our lives and how we begin to listen to our hearts and our bodies!

It can be very easy for our HEAD to take over, to get in the way, and to tell us we should be achieving faster, better and stronger in a matter of days!

But, it's time to stop feeling surprised when the all or nothing mentality works against you…again!

Our society is built on quick fixes promising pipe dreams of health, happiness, better sex and weight loss all in a magic bottle … for only 3 payments of $299!

We get sucked in to these schemes because we all want the result faster; it's human nature! But understand that to achieve these things, the work has to come from within!

Let me ask you something:

If you could have your ideal version of your life, body, health, relationship, happiness and wealth by me just clicking my fingers, would you want it?

Would you appreciate it?

Would you be GRATEFUL for it?

And ultimately, would you really be happy?

To me, the journey is more important than the destination!

The journey is where we experience personal growth, a deep level of understanding about who we are, and pride and respect in what we can achieve.

By doing things the quick or easy way, we don't grow to appreciate ourselves and what we can achieve through sheer grit and determination. We're far less likely to keep our results because we don't have the skills, lessons or education that helped us grow into the person we needed to be in order to live our ideal life!

Ever heard those stories about the lotto winners who found fortunes overnight, only to be in exactly the same place as they originally were three years later?

Their habits, mindset and daily rituals did not support the mass of fortune they had won, so while they may have found some level of happiness in the materialistic gain, they didn't know how to KEEP it, because they hadn't learnt or understood how to live with that sum of money.

So what happened?

They made poor monetary decisions and lost it all again!

In all seriousness guys, we all know that quick fixes don't work, yet we all still want to reach our goals ... tomorrow!

Why?

Because it's more comfortable, we can rely on motivation over dedication, and we don't have to put in the hard yards!

But you know the quick fix isn't the answer, because you've probably tried a multitude of diets before and realised that once you "went back to normal" all the weight piled back on, and the only thing that was lighter was your wallet.

Am I right?

They simply don't work because in order to change, grow and become the person you know you are destined to be, you need to create a NEW normal.

NEW habits, NEW behaviours, NEW thinking styles, NEW mindsets; you have to do what you haven't done before.

It's uncomfortable, it's scary, and you'll be looking at your demons head on and defying them!

Take off the rose-coloured glasses, because you HAVE to go through this process in order to truly succeed long term!

The sooner you come to accept that you're in it for the long haul, the better.

Heck, I've been working on myself at a higher level for the last five years and I know I'm not even close to finished, because I will be working on myself for the next sixty years!

And that shit excites me, not terrifies me!

It's time to stop making rash decisions based on emotion.

It's easy to get sucked in by the noise of others: your friends, your family, advertisements and social media. You judge and compare what you are doing and where you are next to all of these external factors.

It's easy to start doubting ourselves and forget what we have ALREADY accomplished when we see someone reaching their goals quicker, higher and better than what we have (or so it may seem)!

Don't let these emotions get in the way of what you are doing, and remember that what we see and hear every day is more often than not, someone's highlight reel. We don't see the struggles, doubt and insecurities through the TV or our phone screens, so we think that we are abnormal for feeling these emotions ourselves.

But these feelings aren't original or new, they are very, very common.

So welcome to the world's biggest club!

The best piece of advice I can give you in these times of doubt or comparison, is to centre yourself. Take ten deep breaths, feel those negative thoughts wash away, focus on what you have already accomplished, and begin to list all that you are grateful for in your life.

Do this as often as you feel you need to.

But understand that I, myself am the same! It's very easy for our thoughts to run away from us and squash our confidence in a grand total of 0.2 seconds!

The biggest thing I have done to help me through these times is understand exactly when I doubt myself.

What am I doing, seeing or hearing when these thoughts get the better of me?

For me, feeling external noise is completely toxic to what I am doing and the path I am paving, and I compared myself most to other people I know in the same industry.

And when I saw what others were doing, I would instantly start saying to myself "Oh my god, I'm not doing this, or offering that, why aren't I doing this ..."

And instantly my thoughts would get away from me.

When I stopped and centred myself, I could remember and list what I WAS doing and why I was doing it in my own unique way, and simply remind myself that I am not anyone else, and this little lion does not conform ... ever!

I also found one of the best strategies for removing this doubt was to remove the source of the doubt! I unfollowed a lot of accounts on social media so I could control what I saw, and keep my blinkers on to take positive steps forward in my own direction!

Just remember, in order to sustain this new, authentic version of ourselves, we need to adopt a long term approach!

Personal growth is key here. Understand the journey is worth it, because no amount of quick fix magic will ever make us happy, accomplished and fulfilled long term!

ACTION TASK!

In what ways am I suffering burn out, and what is my body trying to tell me in warning?

How can I create some space for myself to refocus and recover before it's too late?

Has my intuition been trying to tell me something lately, but I've been choosing to follow my head instead?

What is the likely outcome of following my head, and not my gut and heart?

How highly do I prioritise sleep, stress management, movement and exercise in my life right now?

What is one small thing I can take action on in each area to create momentum for change?

How would I feel if I made one small improvement to each of these areas after just 1 week?

And how would I likely feel after one month of doing so?

What lessons or experiences am I missing out on by adopting an "all or nothing" approach?

When do I doubt myself most?

In what ways do I feel "noise" from other people or things which makes me doubt my own progress?

How can I reduce this "noise" in my life?

What am I proud of right now?

What do you take responsibility for in your life?

One component which sets apart the dreamers and the doers is how they handle responsibility.

Do you take responsibility for yourself, or throw blame onto others when things don't go your way?

Are you able to look at yourself in an unbiased manner with honesty?

Can you admit your faults, and understand how and where you can make improvements to your life?

Do you focus on the things which will directly help you achieve, or do you worry over the things you cannot control?

These key factors will define what you do, and the results you get from the work you put in.

ACCEPTANCE OR BLAME?

Whether you want to hear it or not (although, you did decide to read this, so in some way you must have known we'd be addressing the "deep shit"!), in order to take charge of your life you need to be willing to take responsibility for the good, the bad and the ugly!

If you're only willing to take credit for the things you've done well, how can you truly propel yourself forward and learn from your mistakes?

In order to enhance your potential, you must be willing to own up to everything in your life: where you are now, where you have been, why you've been held back for years, and your next move forward!

Life will always pay whatever price you ask for it; so if you continue to live in blame or as a victim to your circumstance, prepare to always get the same ol' feelings and the same results. It isn't until you demand more from yourself and accept the past, that you can move forward and ask for a "higher price" in return, instead of settling for lower standards.

The best thing you can do for your own personal development is to admit to the mistakes, then move on! Dwelling on your perceived "failures" won't help you!

What will help is sitting down and mapping out a plan of action to help you if you run into the same or similar problems later down the track. If you haven't owned your shit, prepare to see the same mistakes pop up again and again until you finally say "enough is enough" and look for the lesson!

When you can adopt a mindset where you can take FULL responsibility, you can be truly honest with yourself about where you are now and how you got there! A loser's mentality is someone who thinks they want to change, but pretend they aren't the cause of their own problems!

TRUTH BOMB: We're all the cause of our own problems, BUT, we are also the solution!

Taking full responsibility doesn't mean you have to jump

up and down in public, arms flailing, yelling out to strangers about all the mistakes you've made. No, it simply means acknowledging what happened, why it happened, and finding the lesson in it.

Complete responsibly does require a level of higher awareness in order to take the emotion out of a mistake and simply take the facts from it.

I've had plenty of these in my time, don't you worry about that. But the more experience I've had, the better I've dealt with things.

Instead of looking at myself as a failure, and telling myself a story about "how stupid I am" and "how I can never get anything right", I've looked for the lesson.

The first question I ask myself now when a problem or mistake arises is "What can I learn from this?" and "What can I adapt so this doesn't happen again, or so I can make the situation better next time?".

When you can look in the mirror and offer up complete honesty, you can literally watch your life and your perspective of things transform.

If you are stuck playing the blame game, you'll never truly be able to let go and move forward, and you'll be forever coming up with excuses as to why you can't do X, Y and Z.

Let's start with taking a big long look in the mirror (WITHOUT picking yourself apart) and offer up the following questions to yourself:

Do I understand that I am the only person capable of making ME change? (Nope, no one else can do the work for me!)

Am I willing to take a long look at myself and own up to the habits and behaviours which (deep down) I know are holding me back?

Would I be happy with half results, based on half efforts, or am I ready to go all in?

If you aren't satisfied with your answers, maybe it's time to step up and take full responsibility!

The choice is yours; but stop blaming others for the lack of results you achieve in your life from the work you didn't do.

The truth is, it's HARD to shut out blame and step up to what's happened in our lives.

It's easy and comfortable to pass the buck onto someone else, because that's what everyone else does.

But do you really want to be like everyone else?

Surely, if you've made it this far through the book, it's because you are ready to play the long game and be part of that 5% who refuses ordinary and craves greatness, right?

Another simple mentality you can adopt to help get you started is to remember that life is happening FOR you, not TO you!

What opportunities are you opening yourself up to by admitting your own mistakes and learning from them?

Because everything happens for a reason: to teach us! If we stay closed off and small-minded, we are reducing the possibility for amazing growth and life experiences!

DEFINE YOUR RELATIONSHIP WITH THE CONTROLLABLES

What are the two things in our life we CAN control?

Our thoughts and our actions!

What can't we control?

The weather, the time (hey, it's never slowing down is it, BUT we can learn how to better manage our time!), our genetics, the traffic, and how other people think and behave.

Why do we continue to let the uncontrollables get in our way and stop us from moving forward?
Why do we hang onto these external factors which negatively impact our emotions?
Why do we let poor traffic ruin a perfectly good day?

It's time to open ourselves up to the fact that the uncontrollables are absolutely and completely inevitable! However, they do not define who we are or what we do!
When we run around trying to control every little aspect of our lives, not only do we completely exhaust ourselves, but we try to be so perfect that we become unhappy and unfulfilled. And not only that, we end up driving our loved ones away because we try to control them too!

I spent too much time in my life hanging on to unnecessary shit, and when I was able to let go of it all, it's like I could finally breathe again!
It wasn't until I "checked myself" and realised how these uncontrollables were affecting my mindset that I could move

forward!

I spent so much of my life worrying!

Worrying about why so and so said this, and why they responded in such a way, why I never had any time, and why I couldn't make my clients do the work they were supposed to be doing to get the result they had told me they wanted!

I guess you can see what happened, right?

Complete and utter burn out! I was emotionally drained!

Focusing on these things closed off to my mind to the amazing things that were happening around me. I had built so many great things in my life, but I couldn't stop to enjoy them because I was constantly worried about the next thing on my agenda.

Working in an industry such as this can be tiring. I do get a lot of "emotional baggage" dumped on to me, and I do feel frustrated when my clients don't put in the work to achieve their goals and desires.

But, letting go of control was the best thing I ever did!

It's not that I didn't care; in fact I care very deeply. But in order to do that, I had to care for myself first. And that meant not hanging on to negative shit, and the things I couldn't control, and instead looking at and focusing on all the positives around me:

- A client hitting a personal best in the studio
- A client overcoming a huge emotional block and seeing a weight lift off her shoulders
- Stopping to "smell the roses" and notice what I have achieved

and built from the ground up
- Putting my energy into becoming the best version of myself, so my clients could follow my lead

Yes, I still get frustrated when I see people not following through on my advice and coaching, but one of my biggest lessons has been that if I show up for them everyday, and if I put in my half of the deal (and more), yet they don't want to take action and try to make positive improvements to their life, then I cannot control that.

I can control how I show up for them, and how I can motivate and encourage them. But I can't do the work for them, no matter how badly I want to see them succeed.

The people who are truly HUNGRY for success will follow my lead, and will push me to do even more for both them and myself, to lead them to what is truly possible.

And this shit is powerful!

When I'm in this state, I want to sprinkle glitter EVERYWHERE!

I want to enrich and heal people's lives, and it takes me focusing on my controllables, and not my uncontrollables to do so!

ACTION TASK!

What in your life are you holding onto that is dragging you down?

Is this a controllable or an uncontrollable?

What uncontrollables are you choosing to consciously let go of and move forward from TODAY?

Habits: Do they suffocate or empower your inner lion?

We are the sum of what we do, day in, day out.
What many people fail to realise is that we use habits in over 60% of our daily lives.

To ensure long term success, we must look at our habits!
When we focus on what we should and shouldn't be doing, instead of changing our core behaviours, we will constantly feel like we take two steps forward, and one back. It's not that we are weak, or don't have the desire to change, it's just that our current wiring of behaviour is contradictory to what we truly want!

THE PROBLEM WITH WILLPOWER

The problem with willpower is that we all try to "beat it". (Come on, I know you have at least once in your life!)

We set these personal challenges to ourselves about how long we can refrain from doing something or eating something, thinking that "beating" our willpower is the answer to it all.
But it's not.
And trying to prove a point to ourselves isn't all that productive or healthy!

HABITS: DO THEY SUFFOCATE OR EMPOWER YOUR INNER LION?

With poor habits in our way, no amount of willpower will ever stop us from behaving in a way which is in alignment to our current habit or programming. We like to think that we can be stronger than that, but we aren't.

So, the answer to your question, "Why can't I stay away from that chocolate in the cupboard?", isn't a matter of weakness, but a matter of habit (and proximity)! Yes, the longer the chocolate stays there, the more likely it is to be eaten.

UNDERSTAND YOUR HABITS IN ORDER TO REFRAME THEM

In order to change our habits and behaviours, first we must understand them.

Habits play a critical role in our lives, as we receive millions of pieces of information each and every minute. If it weren't for our habits, menial things like brushing our teeth or driving to work would be extremely complex due to the overwhelming amount of information entering our brain. It would be like having to re-learn how to change lanes, or park our car each and every day.

Exhausting, right?

What happens to all this information we do receive?

Our brains chunk pieces of information together into what's important, not important, and what is a usual routine of ours that we can perform on autopilot in order to free up space for new and different stimuli.

Our habits and behaviours are simply a routine that we perform often, that is easy for our minds to perform due to occurring so often.

Ever driven home and realised once you arrived that you don't remember even driving in the first place?

Yep, that is the work of habit, where our subconscious mind took over and got us from A to B, allowing room for us to think about other things!

Let's take a look at how a habit works in more detail:

The Cue:

In order for a pattern of behaviour to be carried out, our minds need to associate some form of cue as a reminder of what we need to do.

The cue is the reminder for us to then carry out a task.

For example: Each night once you finally get the kids down to bed, you likely turn on the TV to unwind for an hour or so. What often happens when we turn the TV on?

We get the munchies!

On autopilot, up we trot to the kitchen to get ourselves a piece of chocolate or a biscuit.

And every night, as I'm sure you do, you feel annoyed about what you ate, and make a mental note to do better tomorrow night.

Right?

Turning on the TV to unwind is our "cue" to start the pattern of behaviour for getting a snack! And while in the beginning it was probably all very innocent, you began to do it so often that it has become a hard-wired behaviour and something you do without giving it too much conscious thought.

The Routine:

What happens when our brains make an association with a cue?

We carry out the routine on autopilot!

The routine is what we do each time the habit takes place. In this instance, it was hopping up to get something to eat!

The Reward:

The reward is that feeling we get after carrying out the

routine.

Our minds are wired for positive reinforcement. So if we do something once and it feels great (whether it is positive or negative in the long run) we will crave that feeling we get from doing it again.

And what happens when we sit down with a nice piece of chocolate or a biscuit?

Satisfaction!

It tastes nice, we get a rush of endorphins, and we are happy!

What started as simply turning on the TV became something much different, regardless of whether you were hungry or not!

Are you wondering why you are struggling to change long term?

Because the reward for carrying out the pattern is so good, you actually don't have any leverage to change!

So, how do we change this pattern?

We must change either the cue or the routine CONSCIOUSLY, whilst still ensuring we have some kind of positive reward that can develop into a craving.

This is where it becomes really important to be aware of our thoughts and our behaviours, so we can check ourselves when a habit begins. And let me tell you, it doesn't take long to form a new habit. In fact, it's quicker to form a new habit than to correct an old one. Our brain is always looking for pieces of information to chunk together, so if we repeat a pattern, we find that association and can very quickly form a habit before even realising it ourselves!

Whilst still working with the example above, how could we change the routine or cue to this, but still achieve a reward we crave?

For starters, we can change WHAT we eat. Instead of grabbing a processed and high-calorie snack, jump up and turn on the kettle to make a sweet, herbal tea. Or try a piece of fruit with yoghurt (which contains natural sweeteners and sugars). Either of these options will give us our desired reward (satisfaction), but without the guilt!

To change a habit we can also change the cue. Once the kids are asleep, you could sit down in a different room and read a book or magazine, draw, or do something you enjoy!
The cue and the routine are totally different, which in time will form a new habit, however the reward is still positive because we feel accomplished and relaxed by doing something for us.

This understanding of how habits work can be applied to any aspect of our lives. And I encourage you to be more aware of what you are doing, and take notice of any patterns you see that you weren't aware of before!

Another example we could look at here may look like this:

Let's say you want to start a business and you are overflowing with great ideas, however each night when you get home from work you are so worried about making sure everyone else's needs are being met, you forget about your own!
The frustration of not being able to "start" is leading you to grab a glass of wine each night and use it to de-stress while you

help the kids with their homework.

The cue or reinforcement to this current habit is the feeling of frustration at yet another false start.
The routine once you feel this frustration is you head to the fridge and pour yourself a wine.
And the reward is feeling calm and de-stressed.
However, you know this behaviour doesn't serve you long term, because the longer this continues, the more frustrated you are that you aren't getting your own business ideas onto paper.

A new routine could look like this:

The kids grab their homework out and head to the kitchen table. You, armed with a new shiny notebook and pretty pen (nice stationery always helps, trust me!), sit down at the table with your kids.
While they work away, you scribble down ideas and notes regarding your own business to help get you off the ground.
The reward? Satisfaction and a sense of accomplishment for working on YOU while you help the kids too! Not only have you killed two birds with one stone but you feel calmer already because you have taken action without wasting another day not working toward your passion!

Jeanette has also had to learn to recognise how her habit of how she dealt with stress and overwhelm was stopping her from moving forward in her life.
You see, when work began piling up, when the list of things to focus on was getting too much, or when stress began to rear its head, Jeanette would catastrophise. She used to see a big

mountain appear in front of her when things got too much, but instead of dealing with the mountain one step at a time, the negative self-talk would begin, as would the worrying.

In order to feel some sense of control and significance in her life, she would then "unload" or complain to others in order to feel better (whilst ignoring the looming mountain).

For Jeanette, the cue to this bad habit was the stress of work piling up, and feeling pulled in multiple directions. The routine was to turn to catastrophisation and negativity; the reward of which was the feeling of significance and attention in telling others.

In order to change the habit, Jeanette had to change the routine and find a reward which would give her a sense of purpose in a positive way. The cue will never change, as we all have periods of stress and overwhelm in busy times, so we had to focus on the routine.

She began to recognise the patterns of these feelings so she could consciously shift the routine. While Jeanette can still see a big mountain looming over her in these times, she has chosen to change her self-talk, and approach the problem with a solution focus. She sees the mountain, tells herself "You can do this", writes a list, and prioritises her tasks accordingly. Gratitude has also been a big contributor to dealing with how she's been feeling, as she can begin to feel all the things she has already achieved, and this helps to put her problems into perspective.

The new reward for this new habit is no longer significance, but instead achievement. By becoming solution focused, Jeanette has been able to improve her productivity and tick more things off her list than she thought possible. This in turn gives her the confidence to continue to face that mountain and tackle it. So now, instead of hiding from the problem, she can take action on it; and this in turn has helped her feel more in control.

The best way to cement new habits is to link them to an emotion. We can do this by associating them with our "why" or our goals.

"Will doing X behaviour take me closer to where I want to be?"

By asking ourselves this, we will begin to crave the feeling that our habit or behaviour is providing us with: The sense of accomplishment in knowing that each time we complete X task, we are moving closer to our why, which will drive us to reinforce even more positive habits in our lives!

HABITS: THE MAKE OR BREAK

Your habits will make or break you; so what are you willing to sacrifice to get to where you want to go?

Put simply, quick fixes DO NOT WORK long term! So, in order to change, we need to address our thinking styles and thought patterns, not just our daily routines or behaviours!

Yes, how we think is as much a habit as how we behave!

And not all habits are bad. In fact, when we can wire positive habits into our lives, success doesn't become easier, but how we view what's required to succeed does. The more we reinforce positive thoughts and ideas, the more likely they are to become a part of our subconscious programming: our default setting.

If we can allow our subconscious mind to work in alignment with our conscious mind, we will be far more likely to succeed!

How you currently think, act and behave is in alignment with your current programming.

During childhood, we have no conscious thoughts until ages four to six, so everything we know and believe is a reflection of our environment: the people we spent time with (our families) and their behaviours, actions and ideas.

Think about it, is there a certain food you don't like, but you don't know why you don't like it, nor have you even tried it?

I guarantee you don't like it because one of your parents don't like it, so in childhood, you never ate it and were make to believe that it was yuck!

Our wiring is simply a reflection of our childhood, our experiences and the beliefs of our parents, our grandparents, and their parents before that! And when we are wired in a particular way, we will always want to think in alignment with this wiring because it's comfortable (and we all crave comfort).

Now, I'm not to say your parents or loved ones are at fault if you are wired "poorly", because it's simply what they knew at the time. This is why you may have, once or even many times in your life, felt resistance from them if you challenged the families status quo. Not because the decision you were making at the time was bad, but because they didn't feel you valued their ideas and opinions, which is of course a reflection on themselves and their parenting.

Our childhood experiences also shape how we are programmed. The best example I can use now is of the "millennials". Millennials are stereotyped to have been brought up with everything handed to them.

They come last at their athletics carnival? They still get a medal.

They don't like the toy they were gifted? They get to exchange it for something better.

Putting your ideas of parenting aside, how can this type of programming influence a child later in life?

Perhaps they don't see the value in persistence because it has always been easy to win a prize regardless of their performance. Or perhaps they have become so comfortable in believing that everything will go their way, or work out in their favour, that they sit back and wait for opportunity to come knocking, instead of going after what they want.

HABITS: DO THEY SUFFOCATE OR EMPOWER YOUR INNER LION?

Now, I was lucky enough to be blessed with a happy childhood. I was made to feel that I could do or be whatever I want to be, as long as I worked hard for it.

And that I did!

For most of my childhood my main passion was horse riding. So, where would I spend most of my time? Outside, looking after my horse. It was up to me to care for it, feed it, brush it, saddle it up, and train it; and I loved it! I built a lot of resilience from working with some challenging horses along the way.

But, I have also seen first-hand through other relationships within my family, just what can happen when you challenge the status quo. I have watched people trying to prove themselves to someone else their whole life, with no acknowledgement or applause, and it's resulted in them making excuses not to do something they care about, because they know they won't get the reward at the end (which to them was acknowledgment).

This too can be a slippery slope!

REFRAMING OUR SUBCONSCIOUS

So, why should we want to reprogram our thoughts and ideas?
FOR US.
For our inner lion!

Change because you want to change, not because you want to show someone else up, and I can guarantee your life will be happier as a result!
If what you truly want (and the process that you need to take) does not align with your current programming or default, you won't get to where you truly want to go.

The best way to change our subconscious programming is through repetition.
You know why people tell you to "fake it 'til you make it" or "say it until you believe it"?
Because repetition is the key to mastering your sub conscience, and inserting new ideas and thought patterns into it!

Have a think now: what is something you tell yourself often, which is a reflection of what you have grown up believing or hearing someone else say about you or themselves?

Let's say it was "I'm not good enough".

You will spend your whole life living in alignment with the "I'm not good enough" mantra because that's what you believe to be true, so it is now your identity. You've been telling yourself this same story for so long, that every time you don't achieve what you wanted to, you allow "I'm not good enough" to be a valid excuse or reason to not try again and succeed.

Can you see now how a pattern such as this can hold you back from everything you want?
If you don't believe you are good enough to achieve something, why should you?
Because life is just paying you the price you asked for anyway.

How can we use repetition in an instance such as this to insert a new and more positive thought or mantra into our programming?

A thought which will allow us to achieve what we want because we live in alignment with the very idea everyday?

You can make a new mantra, and say it OFTEN!

You could replace "I am not good enough" with "I AM WORTHY OF SUCCESS"!

Do you have to believe it straight off the bat? Nope.
And you probably won't if you've been telling yourself the same story over and over for the last twenty years.
But what you do need to do is persevere, and challenge your beliefs and the very idea of where "I am not good enough" came from.
Yes, you may feel like a fraud in the beginning by inserting a new idea into your mind that you do not yet believe yourself.
But stick with it!
You are going to tell yourself this new mantra so often, that soon enough you will absolutely believe it in your mind, body

and soul!

When should you say this new mantra?
Anytime and anywhere!

We need to keep this new idea of "I am worthy of success" right up in our conscious mind to help it pierce into our sub conscience!

Say it when you are eating breakfast, brushing your teeth, walking the dog, cooking dinner. Say it when you have an important decision to make, one in which your old thought of "I'm not good enough" wouldn't have allowed you to make.

You don't have to say it out loud, but you do have to say it very consciously in your mind to stop the rest of the chatter in your head and leave room only for this thought!

You may even like to find a song which you love, which makes you feel strong and empowered, and play this often too. Every time you play your song, you can associate it with the thoughts and the feelings of being worthy of success!

You could also associate your new mantra with a smell or mood. I love using essential oils as a way of grounding myself and lifting my moods. Whenever I need to, I roll my favourite bottle of oil onto my pulse points which smells of confidence to me.

In time, you will begin to feel worthy, and your old thought pattern will be a distance memory, like a blip in the ocean of your life.

Once your subconscious mind BELIEVES that you are worthy of success, you will begin to live, behave and think as if you are (worthy), and your results will improve ten-fold.

CAREFUL, THE OLD YOU WILL TRY TO COME KNOCKING

There will be times that the old you (your old mantra) will coming knocking at the door to both your subconscious and conscious mind, but don't answer it!

Don't even entertain the idea of it!

It can be very easy for our minds to fall back in to old patterns, particularly if it were something we carried with us for a long time. Remember when I spoke about how it's easier to form a new habit, but harder to lose one?
This is why it's so important to remember your mantra!
Don't give those old thoughts enough time to even creep back in and try to slip a note under the door!

If you do, you can easily fall back into old ways, and doing so will quieten your inner lion.

It's important here to be present with yourself, particularly if you find yourself in a situation where your old "I am not good enough" version of you would have faltered.
These situation will be your hardest, and this is where your new mantra will be needed most. Stay conscious in these situations and keep repeating "I am worthy of success" so quickly and so loudly in your mind, that the "I'm not good enough" bullshit gets no air time.
There is simply no ROOM for this idea to even enter your thoughts when you repeat your new mantra so religiously and so confidently!

You may even wish to play your song in times like this, as this will help to cement your new ideas into your mind!

Remember lion, it's okay to fake it 'til you make it!

ACTION TASK!

What habit is working for me right now? Describe the cue, the routine and the reward of carrying out such habit.

What habit isn't working for me right now? Describe the cue and the current routine.
How can I change this habit?
What are some different routines I can implement which still carry a positive reward?

What is a common thought I have in my subconscious mind?
How has it hindered me in getting to where I want to go?
What would happen if I continue to live by this belief for the next 5, 10, 20, and 30 years?
What pain will recur in my life as a result? (Describe it in detail)

What is a new mantra I WILL enter into my subconscious mind instead?
How will living by this new idea help me succeed?
How will this new idea enrich my life? (Describe it in detail)
What is a thought, idea, song or action I can use to help associate my new mantra?

It's time to find your pride!

The people you surround yourself with, and invest your time into, will have a huge impact on the progress or development you do or do not make.

Understand that we all have an innate need to feel included.

However, staying in a pride of people for the sake of belonging isn't good enough if their values, wants and needs no longer align with your own.

Let's delve deep into this to help you gain an understanding of how prides (or herds) operate, and how you can use them to enhance your success.

THE HERD MENTALITY

Have you ever sat back and watched a herd of animals and how they interact with one another?

If you have, you will see that there are behaviours which are tolerated within that herd, and those which are not.

Certain behaviours will be punished by another animal in the herd as a way to "self correct" and bring the animal back into line.

And if the poor behaviour does not cease?

They are cast out.

Now, this is deeply ingrained and primitive behaviour, and us humans are exactly the same!

In cave man times, this herd mentality served a great purpose: to keep each individual safe and free from danger.

And while we may not be in life or death danger now, herds or prides fundamentally work the same way.

If someone completes a behaviour or action which is not in alignment with the ideals of the group, or which makes another individual uncomfortable, they will be corrected.

This can be good, or it can be bad, depending on the type of pride you are involved in.

If you are wanting to make positive improvements to your life, to reach for more, try new things and take risks, but your group is made up of people who are happy to grind, who don't want to try new things, push themselves, or challenge the status quo, then your behaviour will be corrected. All of a sudden, they will feel threatened. By seeing you do something that is not in alignment with the beliefs of the rest of the pride, you will be confronted for it. Now, before you go blaming your current pride for the nasty things they may have said or done to you, understand that their correcting behaviour can also be subconscious.

Firstly, it will begin with gentle reminders: "Why are you doing that, how stupid", or "Are you going to ANOTHER seminar? What a waste of money!".

Gradually, if you do not come back down to their "safe zone", you'll see more aggressive corrections occur: "You don't value us anymore", or "I'm not sure we can be friends anymore, you've changed".

See what I mean?

Now, when these corrections occur, you have one of two options.

You can either retract, go back down to the level of your herd and continue to feel unhappy and unfulfilled.

OR

You can find a new herd; a herd with values which align with yours, and who exhibit behaviours of the person you hope to become.

This corrective behaviour doesn't always have to work against us. It can work for us too.

When you are part of a higher quality pride, the individuals will feel uncomfortable when you become complacent, or stop reaching for your own goals and personal growth. So, they will begin to drag you UP (not down), in order to give you the push you need to continue.

Now, I'm not saying that you should leave all your friends and never speak to them again, but understand that we all have a deeply ingrained need to belong. We want to feel like we are a part of something, we want to feel valued and respected, and we want to please others.

If your pride is not giving you the room you need to change your life, it's time to find a new one! Otherwise, you will continue to go in frustrating circles for the next 2, 5, or even 10 years to keep everyone else but yourself happy.

In order to move forward, you need to look after you. And that may be that you decline the next lunch catch up and instead choose to have coffee with a mutual friend who has just started their own successful business. Or perhaps you head to a yoga class to surround yourself with some more calm, rather than chaos.

The more time you spend with the right people for you, the more you will crave working to become the person you WANT to become.

Choose the time you spend with people wisely, because their words have the capacity to inject self doubt and rejection into your mind. And let me tell you, these are not productive thoughts to help you succeed.

HOW TO FIND A PRIDE WHO LETS YOU BE AUTHENTICALLY YOU

Something I have come to learn myself is I need to be unapologetically "selfish" when it comes to my visions for the future.

For a long time, I felt like there was something wrong with me, or that I pushed people away in order to fulfil my goals. I put a strong value on my time, and understand what is going to help or hinder my progress. If I need to decline a dinner catch up for some mental health time on the couch, I'm not sorry about it, because I know that I will wake the next day fresh, energised, and keen to go again! What I have come to realise is that this doesn't make me a bad friend, or a rude person just because someone else thinks so.

When I have the right people in my herd, they don't make me feel bad for saying "No".

Instead, they understand. They know I value their time and friendship, but they also understand that I am headstrong when it comes to my sense of achievement, my own development, and my goals. Not only this, but what I do and the help I give to others can be emotionally taxing, and at times after a big week, all I want to do is Netflix and chill, and that's okay!

It's time to find your own pride or herd who helps you be unapologetically you, too!

You will feel free, you will feel confident, and most of all, you will feel safe.

You won't feel like you need to risk losing their friendship in order to work on you.

There will be no back-handed complements, no digs at what you are doing, and most of all, you will feel encouraged to push harder and inspire them to do the same.

Social media makes us feel that we need to belong to a "squad" to know we've made it. The squad mentality tells us that we need fifteen to twenty friends, that we should all be taking exotic holidays together, and that the rest of us, with our three to four close friends are not enough.

In reality, it's extremely difficult to find twenty people who totally get us; who understand us, who share our values, and who can help us in times of need.

This is something I have battled with immensely, feeling like I don't have many friends, and wondering what was wrong with me.

Newsflash! There was NOTHING wrong with me, but there was everything wrong with the unrealistic expectations placed on us all.

I can count on one hand the incredible people who are in my inner, inner circle. The people I confide in, who help me, who support me, and who don't think my vision is too wild. It's taken me a long time to find these people, but I'm so grateful I have.

And in finding my own herd like I have, it has pushed me to ensure I create the same, high quality herd within my business community so all my members feel part of something bigger than themselves, who feel comfortable to be them, and who can have fun and laugh with each other on their quest to becoming their best selves.

What do you need to do to find a pride like the one I'm describing?

To start with, you absolutely WILL need to get out of your comfort zone and meet new people.

We all fear being rejected, but what if the rejection you have faced up until this moment leads you to connecting with the people you were supposed to find all along?

If you are on the journey of personal growth, it's important to put yourself out there. Find people on a similar path, or those who have done what you want to do, so you can model them.

There is nothing wrong with asking someone how they did something, or the steps they took to achieve X, Y and Z!

The right people are the ones who want to help you succeed, and from my own personal experience, mentoring someone and helping them achieve their own success is both empowering and fulfilling! Heck, I feel chuffed if someone wants to ask my advice or opinion, or wants me to share my story with them.

Can you think of someone in your life, someone you know through association, or someone you've been watching from a distance, who you want to get to know and want to hear to their ideas?

Well, take them out for a coffee!

People will give you more time and assistance than you think IF (and only if), they can see you are committed to the hard work and the journey that lies ahead!

Achievers respect and admire other achievers; it's that simple!

By getting out of your own way, randomly messaging that person you've been admiring, and asking them for their time, you could uncover something truly incredible!

It can show you what it means to be surrounded by people who want to excel, work hard and commit to being their best selves. And the empowerment comes from finding someone, or a few people, who you can connect with.

Stop sitting on your hands and ask the awesome girl boss for a coffee for christ sake!

Or attend that seminar you are interested in.

Go to a workshop on your own.

Enter an environment where the types of people you want to associate with would be, and watch them interact!

As I said before, it isn't about unfriending your current pride and never seeing them again.

It's about putting a high value on you, your growth, and what you need to achieve it.

If you crave an intellect conversation, go and find it! Don't try to force it out of your current circle of friends, knowing full well they'll think you need to check in to the looney bin (trust me, been there)!

Are you willing to risk some rejection to find connections with people who will help to propel you up?

HOW MUCH ARE YOU WILLING TO TOLERATE TO EITHER RISE UP OR SIT BACK DOWN?

We all have an innate need to belong.
But are you staying comfortable in a herd which no longer serves you, just to hide away from rejection?
I get it; it's rough! No one likes to feel rejected, and we all want to feel part of something.

But how much are you willing to sacrifice in order to belong?

Will you take criticism, negativity, picky comments and the cued eye rolling just to feel like you are in a circle of people?
Because sooner or later, this environment absolutely WILL dim your light and your desire to achieve what you originally set out to.

What price are you willing to put on creating the life you've been dreaming of?

Something my Dad often asks me is "Who's on your bus?"

This analogy always reminds me that people in our innermost circle will come and go.
Sometimes, people will get off at a stop when it no longer serves them, or when they no longer value or like where your bus is headed. But, people will also get on your bus, and if they are the right people, they will stay.
Don't take it personally if someone hops off your bus. It's not you; it's them. Often, the ones who do leave your bus help you to realise that they had an agenda of their own all along, or

perhaps their own visions no longer align with yours.

We can't lock the doors and force people to stay in our lives (and on our bus), as we will only breed resentment. Just like it's okay for people to leave our bus, it's also perfectly okay to kick someone off too; don't forget that.

But, instead of feeling hurt or sadness if someone leaves our lives, find the lesson from each person you meet along the way. Good or bad, they all add value to our lives and help shape us into the person we are today, and who we want to become.

I know first hand how hard it can be to be a part of a lower quality herd, and to feel like they are going out of their way to stop you reaching your goals. And as I said before, a lot of their actions are done out of discomfort and fear, either consciously or subconsciously.

To me, it was never about neglecting these people or suddenly pushing them out of my life; it was about continuing to value them as individuals, but keeping them at arms length when it came to disclosing what exactly I was doing. So, while they were in my life, they were no longer on my bus. While this was difficult at the time, it was essential for me to remove noise and doubt, so I could go forth and conquer.

I guess the question you should be asking is, "Am I willing to choose feeling temporary rejection if it means I will become happier, more fulfilled and paving greatness for myself?"

We can't expect others to change with us, nor should we sacrifice ourselves for the happiness of someone else. If you continue to stay in a cycle of fearing rejection over embracing YOU, you will find yourself self-sabotaging your own results.

You will begin to modify your own behaviour to "fit back in" and justify to yourself that it's better this way, or that you didn't need to change in the first place.

"It isn't that bad" is THE biggest dream killer out there folks!

Yes, perhaps the risk of rejection is much scarier than the effort (and reward) in working toward your goals, but isn't it worth taking a chance on?

DOES YOUR PARTNER WANT TO SEE YOU SUCCEED AS MUCH AS YOU DO?

Relationships take work, they take time, and they take mutual understanding and compromise.

How invested is your partner in seeing you succeed?
How supportive are they of your journey?

Because who you choose to spend your life with is the person that will always stay in your core, inner-most circle.

Most of the time, they will probably know you better than you know yourself, and they will be there through every rollercoaster of emotion you have.

Ensuring they are on your team will be paramount to your success.

And let me tell you, just like within our friendship circles, our partner can struggle or become uncomfortable if we are conquering our own lives, and they are not.

Is the person you have chosen to be with open to personal growth alongside your own?

Even if they are not, will they always be your biggest fan, no matter how uncomfortable they may feel if they don't appear to be moving in the same direction?

Whatever their actions, what they do, they do out of love and protection for you (some just have different ways of showing it)!

The biggest thing to remember is relationships aren't tit for tat. It's easy to fall into these patterns if we are tired, if we have shifted priorities, or if we are trying to juggle and manage our time differently.

Relationships are about compromise and communication.

Yes, there will be times where you will need to pick up the slack for your partner around the house if they are going through a particularly busy period. Then there are times when they will need to do the same for you.

It will come and go in waves, but team work makes the dream work.

Stop feeling frustrated when you get home from work and they haven't yet prepared dinner because they've also had a huge day. Simply take a few deeps breaths, empathise with them, and whip up something easy.

I can't even begin to tell you what a rock my partner has been to me throughout the whole journey of opening my own business, building my studio, and the time I have invested into weekends of self development and learning (often leaving him home to look after the fur babies). And this is all while running his own company, too!

I wouldn't be where I am today if it weren't for his unwavering support!

Not once has he kicked up a fuss about my working hours, or the state of the house, he just understands that what we do is our own version of normal. But he also knows how to check me and pull me up if I am getting ahead of myself (which I often do!), and reminds me to think about what is important right now, prioritise my tasks, and refocus!

Over the years, I have come to understand that his way of

showing support is to help me look at the cold hard facts. In the beginning, I used to feel like he wasn't supporting me when he wanted to talk about the logic, the potential outcomes, and any other consequences or costs which may appear in my conquests. What I have grown to learn is that this is his communication style, and also his way of protecting me. I now know that Jase would do anything in his power to help me succeed; it just came down to understanding how we each communicate, and consciously stopping myself from feeling defensive or attacked when he wanted to talk the facts and figures.

For one of my dear friends, Trish, her partner has been loving, accomodating and supportive in every avenue she wishes to pursue (her latest being her physical and emotional transformation). He would move mountains to see her succeed, but also understands that she is fiercely independent, so he encourages from the sidelines, confirms her decisions with a "go get it" attitude, and only jumps in where he needs to.

Trish has come to understand the way in which her partner communicates with her and supports her. Yes, sometimes the odd comment stemming from jealousy will slip out, but Trish uses what she has learnt as a way to help him find his own way on his journey too.

Talk about an inspiring and beautiful relationship, right?

What you will find is your partner has their own unique way of showing support to you, you just have to put your detective hat on and find out what it is!

But we will never be perfect, we will make mistakes and we will say something we don't mean, but the important thing here is that you learn from it, and think about what emotion your action was coming from, then communicate it to your teammate.

I think the important thing to ask yourself here is (in total honesty), how can I make improvements to my relationship?

How can I communicate with my partner so they understand what I am doing, what I want to do, and why?

Is my partner saying and doing things out of love and protection (even if they don't have the best way of going about things)?

Am I meeting my partner's needs, as well as my own?

And, is my partner my biggest cheerleader?

ASKING FOR HELP ISN'T A SIGN OF WEAKNESS

One of my old, debilitating beliefs was that vulnerability was weakness.

I used to believe that feeling emotional, frustrated or upset told the world that I was not strong

"Who am I to be a leader if I am weaker than those who follow me?", I would ask myself.

I would disconnect from those closest from me so they didn't see me as the weak person I thought I was. I wouldn't reach out for help when I needed it, because I thought I could manage on my own. I would then enter a vicious cycle of frustration and emotional exhaustion!

Sound familiar?

I know a lot of women out there feel like they are "carrying" their families, or those around them.

Everyone leans on you and expects you to take on their problems because you're the "strong one". You fear showing people your true feelings for risk of criticism because you don't want to be labelled as the weak fraud you believe you are!

Well, I'm here to tell you that it's perfectly okay to need help, and it's okay to feel like this too.

But continuing down this path of belief is definitely not okay. In fact, it will breed bitterness toward the ones you care for most.

It's time to be honest with yourself, and ask for help when you need it most.

The best way to do this is through practice!

I used to find it very difficult to say "yes" when someone offered help. I would feel guilty that I was burdening them, given they probably had a lot to deal with too.

But this is the difference between being in a herd who love and support you, and being in a herd surrounded by "me" people.

The pride who cares about you and loves you will drop whatever they are doing if they know you need a hand. No questions asked, and no agenda.

And this love, my friend, is what makes us strong!

Disconnection and putting on a persona that you have it "all under control", does not.

The strongest women I know say it like it is, wear their hearts on their sleeve, and aren't afraid to be open about how they feel. This allows us to connect with others, because the people in your team want to see you succeed, want to be a part of your journey, and want to help you so you can live to your highest capacity!

The next time someone offers you help, say "Yes, please" immediately, before your mind has a chance to catch up!

ACTION TASK!

Who is in my inner circle and why?

What do the people in my herd value?
How do they push me to succeed?
Do their values align with my own?

Who in my herd is not helping me succeed, and why?

Who is on my bus?
Is there anyone on my bus who is no longer there for the right reasons?

In what ways does my partner communicate with me out of love, protection and support? (Remember, these could be perceived as both negative and positive things, so open communication is essential in helping them understand how their way of showing love/protection may not actually help you.)

Overcoming fears: they don't define you

One of the biggest contributors to us NOT going after what we want is ... FEAR!

We overthink, we worry about the worst case scenarios (often when we don't need to), and we question what we are doing and if it really is worth getting uncomfortable for!

How will we know what we are truly capable of if we continue to live our lives defined by the fear that we let hold us back?

Heck, there are many times I've been scared or worried, questioned what I was doing based on the projections of other peoples fears, and doubted if what I wanted was really worth it after all.

I used to ask myself: "Should I just go back to the 9-5 grind, working for the man and bringing home a pay check each week?"

Sure, that would be the easy option for me, but each time I asked myself that, I would shudder at the thought!

The path less travelled is the one I want to lead others down, and I cannot do that by working in a job I'm not passionate about, feeling defined by a job title or assumed hierarchy.

I never closed off possibilities by putting a glass ceiling over my head, and I didn't allow myself to entertain the idea of my "finishing point".

This has allowed me to continue to go forward, proving to

myself with each step that I am capable, and that my potential is only just scratching the surface.

The journey of personal discovery and growth far outweighs any fear which enters my mind, because I know that the best things in life happen on the other side of it!

YOUR COMFORT ZONE IS THE MOST UNCOMFORTABLE PLACE TO LIVE

I know you've heard it before that the magic happens outside of your comfort zone.

This couldn't be any closer to the truth.

Our comfort zones are designed to keep us "safe" and away from danger, but it isn't until you begin to challenge it that you realise how limitless you truly are.

Every action, thought or activity that pushes us out of our comfort zones enables its outer edges to grow just a little bigger each time. With practice, those tasks which once were uncomfortable become easy, and we then feel confidence to level up and push for something a little more.

If you're anything like me, perhaps you write down all the things you'd like to achieve each year on a goal or vision board.

For 12 months, I had something written haphazardly on mine:

"To do something scary"

For a long time, this goal was one with no real merit to it. I knew one day I'd have to face it, but I didn't want to. I just had it written down there to make me feel better about the fact that maybe one day I would, but I wasn't ready yet.

I knew when I finally faced my fear it had to be big and I had to do it with a BANG!

If you haven't guessed it already, this was to be skydiving.

My whole life I had told people they would have to pay me to jump out of a perfectly good plane. But subconsciously, I knew everything I was chasing in my life would happen once I did it.

I was always the over-thinker, and this caused me to say "No" to many opportunities that I craved, but always held myself back from last minute.

When I finally said "Yes" to skydiving, I was able to let go of control, of thinking, and just embrace and be present in the experience.

I knew when I was ready to face this challenge, because what once terrified me at the thought, became something I craved doing for the growth experience. Now don't get me wrong, I was still scared shitless, but ultimately, I was excited for what was to come.

Up in the air, time stood still.

It was peaceful, my worries disappeared, and I was able to let go of all the times I said "No" when inside, I was screaming "Yes"! I can even remember that split second where the transformation took place for me and I replaced fear with exhilaration.

Suddenly, I hadn't died.

In fact, I had never been more alive!

If you haven't done it, I can promise you the apprehension and fear is worth it, and since my first jump, I have taken clients and friends to go through the same experience.

Skydiving made me embrace fear to pursue every avenue of my life, and the things I was holding back from.

Now if something worries me or scares me, I can think back

to that moment and remember that if I can do that, I can literally do anything!

It isn't about becoming fearless, but instead learning to work WITH your fears because the moment I become fearless is the moment I have become complacent. Now, I'm always looking for the next hill to conquer, to allow myself to feel my fears, and survive them, because this is what builds the resilience and mental toughness I need to take each new step.

I'm not telling you that you have to take a leap as big as skydiving to get outside of your comfort zone. You may like to take small steps outside, and that's fine too, as long as you continue to challenge it as frequently as possible, you will reap the rewards of doing so!

As a rule of thumb, if something is both terrifying and exciting, you should definitely do it!

5, 4, 3, 2, 1 ... AND JUST DO IT!

We all want to feel in control of every action (and outcome) we take.

We need to calm the overthinking mind that stops us from doing things out of our comfort zone.

If you continue to question and play that mental debate of "should I do it, should I not do it", you'll be too late and have missed the opportunity that was presented to you!

I spent so many years missing out on things all because I was scared. I would analyse the potential outcomes before even experiencing it for myself, and of course, my mind always went to the worst possible scenarios!

Now if there is something I need to do, the first question I ask myself (and the one which nips the run-through of bad scenarios in the bud) is "But will I die?"

Will I die if I say "Yes" to this experience or opportunity?

Will I die if I screw up my presentation and don't quite hit the mark?

Will I die if I go to the party where I don't really know anyone?

The answer is NO!

When I thought about it, if death is the worst possible outcome and is unlikely as a result of experiencing a particular opportunity, then why shouldn't I do it?

We need to say "Yes" to things before we give ourselves time to say "No"!

Adopt the 5, 4, 3, 2, 1 … ACTION mentality!

By counting down from 5 and just DOING IT, you remove the space in your mind to overthink and run away with any potential negative outcomes because you are too busy consciously counting down and preparing for action!

Even if you don't adopt the count down method, you can try to repeat a phrase or word over and over in your head, as this too allows no room for any other thoughts to emerge.

In September of 2018, I went along to possibly one of the most life-changing events I have experienced; a Tony Robbins seminar.

For those of you who don't know who Tony Robbins is, you've clearly been living under a rock and should definitely Google him!

For those of you who do, you will know that I put myself through the most uncomfortable, fun, incredible, tiring and liberating events I could have ever been to, and we finished Day 1 by walking through fire!

A large portion of Day 1 was spent pumping ourselves up, visualising the walk itself, gaining confidence in our own abilities, and reshaping our beliefs.

We spent plenty of time in a "power pose". A "power pose" or any strong, dominant pose not unlike the Wonder woman pose, has been scientifically proven to increase our confidence when held. Any time I feel I am lacking in confidence, or I'm shy or nervous, I'll head to a quiet place (or a bathroom stall) and hold this pose. Sure, I may have felt like an idiot at first, but no one can see me anyway!

This can be a tool you too can adopt when you have a big

decision to make, when your mind is fighting with you to say "No", or when you need an extra little boost of confidence!

Similar to the countdown approach, we geared ourselves up for our fire walk by repeating the words "cool moss" in our minds. They might sound like random words, but they tricked our conscious minds in thinking that what we were walking on was COLD (yes, when I stepped out onto the coals they FELT cold!), and the words filled any voids in our minds so no ounce of doubt, questioning or fear could enter.

I have used this funny phrase a few times since in moments of fear; both when I went to get my first tattoo, and when I faced my fear of rollercoasters! Not only does "cool moss" distract me from any other thought or idea I might have, but it also reminds me of all I have achieved (like fire walking), when I BELIEVED with every fibre of my being that I could!

Perhaps you have a funny phrase or key word you might like to design for yourself in times of fear, or you may stick to counting down from five. Whatever you decide, it just has to be powerful enough to fill any space in our minds to allow us to take action!

But be careful, you may just love how it feels to remove overthinking, let go of control, and have FUN!

Shock horror: you may even enjoy yourself!

Now, how terrible would that be?

THE TYPES OF PERSONAL FEAR: WHO AM I IN THIS?

One of THE biggest things which holds us back is the different types of fear which plays with our minds.

It stops us from saying "Yes" to that promotion, to starting up our own business, to taking a leap of faith and trying something new, and ultimately, from unleashing our lion within!

The three key areas of fear I wish to focus on here are:

The one who fears failure
The one who fears success
and
The one who feels like the imposter or fraud

You could be one of these fears, or you could be multiple. Chances are at some point in your life, you will experience all of them, and these are the factors which inhibit us from achieving our desired successes (either directly or indirectly). So, I want to run through each of the types of personal fear so you can gain an understanding of them and know what to watch out for when each one rears its ugly head.

THE ONE WHO FEARS FAILURE

Fear of failure is probably the most common fear in all of us.

And unfortunately, it holds us back from saying "Yes" to opportunities, to trying new things, and from uncovering what is truly possible for ourselves!

When we fear failure, we are so focused on what could go

wrong, that we forget about what could actually go right!

Do you worry about looking like an idiot?

Or being judged for not getting it right?

Or is it that your own expectations are so ridiculously high, you know you'll never measure up?

We are so concerned with failing, that we stay in this state of "analysis paralysis" where we overthink, but never actually try or achieve!

So, what do we need to do?

We need to reframe our relationship with failure!

What does failure mean to YOU, specifically?

Because often when we think about failure, we think of the worst case scenarios to us. And even when we make one tiny mistake, our minds automatically scream "Abort, abort, failure is looming!", without giving us a chance to assess what happened and try again!

What is YOUR version of failure?

What are you willing to deem a failure versus deem a learning experience or minor speed bump?

For me, failure is nothing less than giving up!

Any other mistake I make, step I miss, or time I "think" I look like a fool, are simply lessons.

In fact, every "failure" I've had in my life has been an excellent growth opportunity. They've allowed me to think about what happened, without blame or bias, and assess what I need to do next time, to prevent the same thing from occurring again

OVERCOMING FEARS: THEY DON'T DEFINE YOU

This in itself is an excellent opportunity.

However, if I give up and quit because things get too hard, then damn straight I've failed!

By reframing what it means to "fail", I immediately remove expectation and fear, because I know that a stumble isn't the worst case scenario, so I can confidently try new things, knowing full well I'm learning and growing as I go.

And really, if we take a leap, don't make it, and people laugh at us or judge us, are they even the people we want and NEED to hang out with anyway? Or, if in the situation where we didn't know them at all, then why does it matter what a stranger thinks (you're likely never going to see them again anyway)!

If you can decide, right now, that failure to you means giving up, then everything else that happens to you is a gift of opportunity and growth!

If you could do this, you would take the risks when they mattered, and you would stop worrying about what other people think, and instead be applauded by those who matter to you for giving it a crack!

If we continue to fear failure, then how can we allow ourselves to be a beginner at something, so we can learn a new skill which will help our development and growth?

If we want something bad enough, should we try it once, and if we get it wrong, throw in the towel completely?

No, we keep practicing!

Remember when you were learning to ride a bike as a kid?

Sure, you fell down, you lost your balance, and you had trouble steering. But each time you did, you got back up again and persevered until you had mastered the skill.

These days we just don't have the patience or the gusto to be a beginner again, and it's stopping us from achieving our dreams!

These fears towards failure are learnt behaviours.
We aren't born with the fear of tripping over, making a mistake, or getting something wrong on the first attempt.
Instead, these fears are learnt behaviours and reactions to a story we have given ourselves over an event which has occurred in our lives.

I've witnessed many incredibly, talented women wash away opportunity for fear that they won't live up to their own expectations. It pains me every time.
They get so caught up in the "What ifs" that they neglect to realise the amazing gift they will receive if they just get in and have a crack.
This fear dulls our ability to be driven by the instinct of our inner lion. Instead, we allow the self doubt, the worry, and the anxiousness over potential outcomes dull our passion, dull our inner voice, and squash our dreams.

We could all do with living a little more like Richard Branson - by saying "Yes" first, then worrying about the details later!

Take a moment to visualise how your life will look in five years time if you continue to live in the fear of failure.
You didn't get that promotion, or start that business, did you?
You didn't achieve that goal you had your heart set on, did you?

OVERCOMING FEARS: THEY DON'T DEFINE YOU

Ask yourself, "What would future me say to myself if I say 'No' to this opportunity, or don't try X, Y or Z out of fear?"

Would you be happy or disappointed in your current self?

Yeah, I get it, it's hard!

But, it's time to stop letting your past define what you are capable of now.

We've all felt the burden of disappointment when we hold back from something we truly want, because we play "sliding doors" for the next month, wondering about what COULD have happened if we'd just said "Yes".

What would your lion do?
They'd fucking pounce!
They would hunt!
They would go for it, regardless of fear.

THE ONE WHO FEARS SUCCESS

Failure is familiar.

At some point in our lives, we have made mistakes, stumbled, and taken the wrong path. It can be easy to justify "failing" because for some of us, it is so hard-wired into our minds!

But what about success?

Have you ever truly succeeded at something you had your heart set on?

Is the thought of actually succeeding a little daunting?

Do you worry about what people may say if you truly

succeed?

At some level, we fear success. We fear the expectations of ourselves and others when we reach a certain point, and we fear alienating ourselves from our friends and family if we appear to have "made it" and they haven't.

Suddenly, we have set this bar so high for ourselves that we fear we won't be able to maintain it!

Can you see how this can begin to interrelate with having the right or wrong tribe surrounding us?

Success is unfamiliar to a lot of us, so the closer we get to our goals, the more we begin to sabotage our own results because we crave fitting in, not standing out from the crowd.

It's uncomfortable to be seen. When we feel that watchful eye of people around us, we worry about what they say, what they think, and allow the doubt to creep into our minds.

Sound familiar?

With the prominence of Tall Poppy syndrome in this country, sometimes our success and our accomplishments can feel like burdens, not triumphs.

If you are not familiar with the term "Tall Poppy syndrome", it is used to describe how cultures or people resent or criticise those who are deemed too successful or of a higher status. In Australia in particular, people try to cut others down for their achievements whether they flaunt their success or not, and this means we aren't often celebrated for the good we do, no matter how hard we worked for it.

I've felt the weight of this myself, many times!

I've felt like people are threatened by me, that they're jealous of me, and that they're waiting for me to fuck it all up so they can prove me wrong and say "See, I told you she was nothing special."

You are not alone in feeling this way either.

But we have to ask ourselves, is the pain of judgement and the opinions of sheep worth throwing our dreams away for?
Should we really be shooting ourselves in the foot before we've had a chance to see what truly is possible?
Really?

Success takes practice!
It's like learning to ride a bike in the example I used previously. The more you achieve, the easier it becomes to squash those negative thoughts and continue to rise up!
And just like the subconscious mindset I spoke about in previous chapters, we can wire ourselves for failure or for greatness.
Which default are you actively going to choose?

Another reason we may fear succeeding is because we worry the success won't last.
Heck, how many one-hit wonders have there been? Or everyday people who broke the internet one day, and were nobodies again the following day?
Social media has a lot to blame for our fear of success. We don't want to be that chick people talk about as the one who "peaked too soon", then threw it all away.
We all pity people like that, so we worry what our own

success will do to us.
Will it be worth it?
Will it last?

So, how can we reframe success in our minds in a positive way?

We can stop looking at success as a temporary feeling to latch on to, but instead as an everyday habit, and way of life! Success doesn't have to be something we fear, or something we believe we will lose friends over.

If we can demand just 1% more from ourselves everyday, every week, and every year, suddenly success isn't so scary after all. Instead, it can be viewed as something very attainable, and a feeling that can become hard wired as our new normal.

It's also important to remember that "success" is unique and different to everyone. It can be easy to put the term "success" up on a pedestal and fantasise about Lamborghinis, mansions and giant house parties. But this does not define success to the everyday person, and of course we resent this ideal when it becomes less about how we feel, and more about what we own.

It's important to identify what your version of success looks like to YOU at this time in your life. It's unlikely to be mansions and fancy cars, so what are you really so worried about if what you seek to achieve is going to bring you more happiness, health and love?

Our success can open up so many incredible experiences in our lives, if we just have the courage to go after what we want!

Ask yourself, "What opportunities, and what lifestyle will

my success allow me to do and live each day?"

Is it worth the pain and sacrifice?

Because I can assure you it is.

You don't want to just EXIST, do you?

And if people criticise you, find new people! Build a pride of people who love you, and who want to see you become your best possible version of you. Stop holding on to the opinions of those who don't matter, and who you don't even know.

I can guarantee if they're already haters before you've even started to achieve great levels of success, you certainly won't be able to sway them later when you truly are successful (they'll be too proud for that, trust me)!

Whatever you want to do, be or accomplish in your life, know that you can.

You just need to drown out the fear, the doubt and the worry. Stop labelling yourself and defining yourself by what you think others will say about you.

You're doing it for you, not them anyway!

THE ONE WHO FEELS LIKE A FRAUD

Do you feel like you live your life as a sheep dressed in lion's skin?

The classic "imposter syndrome" is a real fear: the fear of being found out to be the fraud you believe you are.

This causes us to feel as though we don't deserve the success and achievements we have made for ourselves. The feelings of low self worth and Tall Poppy syndrome combined, dulls our gratification in our own achievements, and make us feel that perhaps we didn't work hard enough, or sacrifice enough, to be at the higher level we are at.

If we feel we will be shamed or questioned for our success, we will feel undeserving of it. And this is where I feel the correlation between imposter syndrome and Tall Poppy syndrome come into play.

I can tell you, this fear has been the one which has been most prominent for me in the past!

I built my own business quickly, and developed a big client base over a short period of time, which left me questioning:

"What did I do to deserve this?" and "Am I really worth these people's time and money? What if I don't get them the results they wanted?"

These fears were real, and were amplified by the fact that other people around me liked to downplay my success.

I have heard way too many times that my success in my business is a result of living in a small town, because there was less competition.

Ha!

In fact, small towns can be harder to break into because everyone knows everyone, and relative to their size, there is, in fact, more competition. I just happen to be different, and to have built a family feel community that people want to be a part of.

"If the people close to me don't value my achievements, then how can this success be real? And how can I be worthy of it if they don't believe I am?"

The innate feeling of needing to belong is what fed my insecurities of being a fraud.

When I could look at the facts, I found that I could quieten the voice of the imposter in my head because I knew what I was saying to myself (and what I was hearing) was not true at all! (And I had a whole lot of blood, sweat, long hours and sacrificed weekends to prove it!)

So, I didn't give up, and I didn't throw in the towel.

Instead, I decided not to play into these STORIES, and I chose to stop letting these opinions define my worth, because I knew they didn't, and I had plenty of happy clients to prove it.

When you suffer from imposter syndrome, the best thing you can do is put your blinkers on!

Block out the noise of what other people are doing, stop comparing yourself to anyone else, and go about building the empire that is your life.

It doesn't matter if the person next door has a better sale on than you, or that your neighbour gets more likes on social media.

Our inner imposter feeds off self doubt, so the sooner you can squash that, the better!

It's also important to be aware of the expectations you place on yourself.

Do you compete with yourself to the extent that if you don't achieve a target by X date, you are undeserving, or not good enough?

Manage your expectations and stay realistic!

If it takes you a week longer than anticipated to complete a task, it's okay. It doesn't mean you are stupid; it simply means that some tasks take longer than others, and this is something you can learn from. Sometimes we hit roadblocks, or family emergencies appear which we have to deal with, which, in turn, causes us to have to juggle multiple balls. This doesn't make us a failure or a fraud.

In fact, it makes us human.

Are there particular times when you are feeling unworthy or undeserving?

Take a look around, look at what you have created, at what you have achieved, and at how you have contributed to others and enriched lives.

The facts are written there, not in your head!

Start to look for patterns in the emergence of your inner imposter.

Is it just before completing a big project at work?

Or when someone you know achieves a goal they've been working at?

Is it just before you jump in to learning something new?

If you can find the pattern, you can pre-empt and squash those stories in your head before you have a chance to believe them!

How?

By examining the facts.

Just remember, a lion doesn't walk around feeling unworthy. No, it hunts for what it wants with pride!

ACTION TASK!

What version of personal fear do I live in?

What is the possible outcome for me if I continue to live in this fear for the rest of my life? Would that bring me happiness or heartache?

What would my life look like if I didn't live in this fear?

What's the worst possible thing that that will happen if I don't succeed?

Who do I feel I need to prove myself to? And who do I compare myself to most? (Why?)

How can I make myself proud and remind myself that I am doing this for ME?

Letting go and taking back your power

Now that you've made it this far, it's time to start to find a way to believe in yourself, to see that you have the capability to achieve so much more, and to become proud of the person you are, and your inner lion which is beginning to shine through.

LIONS DON'T BOW AS SERVANTS TO THEIR INNER CRITIC

One of the first, most essential steps in transforming your own life, is changing your relationship with your inner critic. How you feel about yourself and the stories you tell yourself have the capacity to ensure you either never have the confidence to go after what you want, or that you do so in amazement to those around you, all with your ego in check!

How you speak to yourself is a both a habit and a deeply ingrained behaviour carried over by thousands of generations to keep you "safe".

Once you can understand that difference between the two, you'll be able to see patterns in how you think, and choose how you respond to them.

For a lot of people, their relationship with themselves has meant that they speak down to themselves, or negatively about themselves, and have done so for a number of years.

Or sometimes, without realising, it's the people closest to us who hurt us the most, and it is their words we hear which we believe as our own.

Most people beginning their journey to deeper levels of mindfulness and happiness are unaware of the impact these thoughts are having, or that they even exist, because they are so normal to them.

What does your inner critic say to you? That you're hopeless, or stupid, or fat, or unworthy?

These negative thoughts have the power to directly affect our level of success or failure, because if what we believe about ourselves and what we truly want are in conflict, we will continue to go around in circles!

Our inner critic is really just projecting an old version of ourselves, or a story we believe about ourselves!

How do you speak about yourself?
How often do you talk down to yourself?
What do you say to yourself when you look in the mirror?
Whose voice do you hear when you criticise yourself? Is it yours,
or someone else's?

Chances are, if you look in the mirror and the first thing that springs to mind is something negative, then you talk this way often, without realising.

If on the other hand, you look in the mirror and give yourself a high-5 or consciously adopt a positive thought, you are well on your way!

This is not about being "self absorbed" in any way. The status quo says that it's shameful to love yourself and to think you're awesome.

Let's challenge this shall we?

'Cause if you don't love yourself, then who's going to?

Cue the eye rolling.

Yes, I saw it.

I know your partner loves you, your family loves you and your best friends love you. But the capacity to strengthen all these relationships comes from you loving yourself, too.

When you love yourself, you have so much more to give to those around you because your head is clear of negativity and you are in a much, much happier place.

Now, the first trick to get you in the right direction is to be consciously aware of your thoughts.

As you know, it takes three weeks or more to form a new habit, so what I want you to do over the coming weeks, is to be conscious in what you tell yourself when you look in the mirror each morning.

If it's negative, actively shut it down.

Don't accept the thought and instead tell yourself one thing you do like about yourself. This can be a physical feature, or it can be a feature of your personality. Whatever it is, make sure only positive thoughts stay in your conscious mind when you're in front of the mirror.

By all means, if you don't yet believe you have any positive qualities, or any love to give to yourself, then fake it 'til you make it!

Verbalise it out loud; if you say it aloud rather than in your mind, this will be more effective in piercing through your subconscious mind to create new default settings. If you feel you need some visual aids to help you, pop up some post-it notes around the house, or on your mirrors, which contain positive affirmations or things that you love about yourself. These constant reminders can help you when you feel stuck, or on the days where you find it harder to be kind to you.

This is by no means an easy task, but it's essential for you moving forward.

You need to become accepting of who you are: your quirks, your strengths and your weaknesses because combined they create one incredible human being: YOU!

Once you have this habit under control (being the story you tell yourself about the person staring back at you in the mirror), the next task is to understand those deeply ingrained behaviours that are buried in our subconscious minds and designed to keep us safe.

As humans, our minds are wired for comfort and protection. However, when we want to unlock deeper levels of our potential and push forward, we need exactly what our minds are designed to resist: discomfort!

Our minds will always want to think in harmony with our subconscience, so when we do something scary, uncomfortable, or new, self doubt will be more likely to appear.

What I have come to find is the closer we get to our goals and dreams, the more prominent these voices will be. I always know I am making progress in the RIGHT direction when I hear limiting words run through my ears: "You aren't good enough", "You aren't worthy of this", and my favourite: "Who are you to deserve to achieve this?".

As much as these voices in our heads can be something we GIVE power to, I've switched my perception and allowed them to give power to ME instead. I have come to understand that when I hear these, I must be moving forward toward the success I crave, and the discomfort I need to experience to get there. So now, when I hear those hateful words in my ear, I can laugh to myself, knowing that soon enough I will prove that girl wrong, again!

For me, over the course of this book I have had my low points, when that inner critic of mine has whispered in my ear that I'm not good enough, or qualified enough to succeed in this. I have had to train my mind that as quickly as these thoughts appeared, I squash them and push them out!
Dwell on them, and they would begin to penetrate through the subconcious programming I have designed for myself, and the old, insecure Zoe would begin to emerge.

I spoke earlier about how our old wiring has a way of rearing its ugly head. This was one of those times for me, and you have to be ready to shut the door and not let it in; because it's easy for our minds to associate old habits or patterns, and if we allow them, they will re-enter our programming.

I'm not going to lie to you and tell you it's easy to shut these voices out; it's not. It takes a high level of courage and confidence to say "No".

As hard as it was, and still is, I just don't let them win. I try to rationalise what I'm hearing, to find the truth in those hurtful words.

And you know what?

There is no truth in what my critic tries to tell me.

I know my inner critic is my old default setting, and I refuse to live a life justifying it. I didn't find happiness in it then, so how would now be any different?

Something which has helped me immensely in looking for the truth in my inner critic's words is by creating a gratitude folder, and by speaking to those closest to me in my inner circle (the women I know who will always pick me back up, and never allow me to quit).

I received the idea of this gratitude folder from a beautiful friend of mine. Crystal, if you are reading this, thank you!

Whenever I receive kind, thoughtful and thankful messages from my clients, friends and family, I screenshot them and save them in my phone. In those moments of self doubt, I have something tangible to remind me of why I do what I do, how I have been able to help and empower others, and why I want to share my message to you all.

When I have real, written words disproving that annoying voice of my inner critic, I have no option but to shut it out, because I can see the truth from others!

Now, I want to tell you a story about an incredible client of mine. At the time of writing this, this client has been with me for two years.

Erin had always been a bigger girl, and a yoyo dieter.

Since working with me, she has managed to educate herself on good quality nutrition, and understands how to fuel her body well, and that eating LESS isn't the answer.

She was training three to four times per week, eating very well, her stress was under control, we had worked through some pre-existing health conditions, and her water intake and sleep were all great.

She achieved great results in her first twelve months, but we just couldn't seem to break through the plateau after that! It was like she was stuck, but on the surface, had no reason for her results to be slowing.

We had always had conversations about the people she spent time with.

Her friends and husband were extremely supportive and helped her, however her mum had always judged her on her weight. She had always openly picked her apart in front of other people, and the main topic of conversation within the family was weight, who was looking good, who was doing what diet, and who needed to lose a few.

Erin often downplayed the implication these thoughts had on her, and easily brushed them off. However, one day, when I asked how she was feeling, I reached her at a particularly low point, and she opened up to me.

Erin told me that she lives in this state of mind that she is "fat".

Each day, she looks down at herself and tells herself she is fat, at least twenty times throughout the day!

Even though she was taking all the right steps forward to change her body, this limiting belief was stopping her from achieving, because it was not in alignment with what she truly wanted!

We dug a little deeper and I asked Erin who's voice it was telling her she was fat.

And guess what?

It wasn't her own voice, but instead the voice of her mum, standing in front of her and picking her apart, just like she had always done in reality.

You see, Erin had been told this so much throughout her whole childhood, teenage years, and into her adult life, that it became her default setting.

Of course she would remain "fat" if that's what she told her self each and every day; because her body would always work in alignment with her subconscious thoughts.

So, what did we do?

We worked through Erin's limiting belief of "I am fat" by some powerful visualisations.

What does her life look like in 5, 10, 15 and 20 years if she continues to live with this belief?

How does she feel? Is she happy, sad, depressed?

What does this belief stop her from achieving in her life?

And then, what does her life look like without this belief?

What has she achieved?

How did she feel?

What was her state of mind?

This is a powerful exercise, and one which takes time. But it allowed Erin to see how happy and free she could feel without the limiting belief and inner critic weighing her down, literally!

She labelled this new feeling, the feeling of how she felt when free of the negativity, into "I am happy". This new state of mind was one which she could then go back to, and remember in times of doubt.

This is a process which takes time, as Erin then had to insert this new belief into her subconscious programming. But, when she realised the implication that "I am fat" was having on her level of success and achievement, and on her happiness, there was the leverage she needed to change for good!

Sure, there will always be ups and downs along the way, and this stuff isn't easy as our current reality is a result of us having lived with that limiting voice and inner critic.

However, when you can BELIEVE that you are not defined by these words, and that they don't dictate your present or future, you can take steps forward to break their shackles which are tying you down!

STOP COMPARING YOURSELF TO OTHERS

In order to fully embrace and allow our inner lion to shine, we must stop comparing ourselves and talking down to ourselves.

The only person you should ever compare yourself to is the woman staring back at you in the mirror.

Why?

Because you are not someone else. You don't think like them, you don't look like them, and you certainly don't behave like them.

Also, it's soul draining!

We spend our lives looking to other people for approval, for respect, and for worthiness, whilst forgetting to find it in ourselves first!

It's easy to look at someone else's performance or achievements and instantly discredit our own.

It's easy to forget that they have struggles of their own, too.

It's easy to think that we won't ever make the same achievements of our own.

We spend all our time looking outwards at others, whilst forgetting to look inwards so we can follow our intuition, and find pride in our achievements thus far.

By focusing on what we don't have (yet), compared to someone else, we set ourselves up for failure before we've even begun. We neglect that fact that the people we are comparing ourselves to have also had to reach the same amount of check points as we have. It's just that we compare ourselves to their progress now, which is an entirely different timeline to ours.

We forget about the journey, the lessons and the teachings we need to find along the way, and look only to the end goal which seems, now, impossibly out of reach.

The only person you need to watch from this point forward is YOU!

When you compare your performance to that of yourself, you level off the playing field. You know, deep down, if you could do better, or if you beat that girl in the mirror.

You can begin to credit your own achievements because suddenly, when there is only a bar and standard set by yourself, for yourself, you'll start to feel excited by those wins you have along the way, instead of discrediting them because "that chick on Instagram" achieved it six months prior.

Who do you see when you look in the mirror?

Someone who isn't as good as the girl next to her?

Or a happy, confident lion who is so focused on moving forward, that she doesn't have time to look sideways?

What wins can you credit to yourself along the way?

They don't have to be the biggest and the best; they just have to be meaningful to you! And no, they don't have to be deemed "good enough" to announce on social media either. Any small step in the right direction brings an opportunity for you to give yourself a high-5 and be proud!

What I have created for my own life has been attributed to finally stepping out of the shadow I put myself in.

Lions don't hide away; they stand tall and proud, allowing everyone to watch them shine!

Like I mentioned earlier in the book, the best way to overcome feeling as if you need to compare yourself, is to unfollow social media accounts which make you feel bad, to help you "block out the noise".

If I feel like I begin to question what I'm doing, and why, I know that I'm letting too much external noise into my head. I let myself watch what others are doing in case they're doing something I "should be" doing, too.

But for me, this is playing with fire.

I don't thrive on following the crowd. Comparing myself to a crowd I don't actually WANT to follow in the first place leads to confusion in my own mind, and stops my creativity from shining!

PAST PERFORMANCE PROGRAMMING

Did you know that we are all programmed to believe what is achievable based on our past performance, and not by what is actually possible for ourselves?

We never ask too highly of ourselves in the off chance we won't meet the performance of our previous attempts, so we dare not stretch ourselves too far, just in case.

I can tell you now, as soon as I lived without a glass ceiling lingering over my head, I opened up a world of possibilities I had not yet imagined for myself.

Suddenly, it didn't matter that I hadn't ever attempted to do X, Y or Z; I just gave it a crack anyway. As soon as we base our possibilities and our limitations on our past, we close off an endless amount of opportunity that we have not yet thought of or created!

Your inner lion doesn't worry about whether she should "give it a try" even though she hasn't before. Instead, she will just get up and do it, because in order to change, and in order to grow into the person we want to become, we need to do what we have not yet done.

Living a life feeling limited by previous actions means we never will try anything new, dare to fail in an attempt, or push ourselves to reach greatness.

It's time to leave all past actions behind and go forward without hesitation, full of confidence, and with a willingness to try something new!

How do we build confidence in ourselves to try new things and break through our own glass ceilings?

We practise!

We push that little bit harder, give it another 1%, and we continue to try new things.

Start off small if you will, but the more often you practise something, and something which you haven't done before, the more confidence you'll find in yourself to tackle anything!

Heck, if Erin (also known as Lil Boss), one of the beautiful coaches at our transformation studio, had relied on her past to dictate her future, there's no way in hell she would be pursuing an avenue such as this for her career. She likely wouldn't have found her "why" either.

You see, Erin grew up with these debilitating beliefs that she was weak, she was lost, she was quiet, she wasn't good enough, and that she was a victim. These beliefs were so hardwired into her that they became her reality.

And when someone she knew, trusted and worked for abused her, she was left feeling totally destroyed.

From that point on, she lived with a feeling of disgust in herself, and fear of everyone around her. She didn't talk about what happened, and instead buried it deep inside.

When the abuser did the same to someone else, she needed to relive everything that had happened to use as evidence, and the healing process could finally begin.

By this time, Erin was working a 9-5 retail job, feeling as though that's all she'd ever amount to. Although she wasn't passionate about her job and what she did for a living, she just believed that that was her normal reality.

Then an incredible transformation took place.

Erin started to rewrite the story she told herself about who she was and what she was capable of, and this helped to pull her out of the hole she was living in. She began exercising, she started to push herself and ask honestly, "What do I want?". She then started to break free of her past programming and limitations. Her healing was a lot of small steps taken, which combined led to a huge breakthrough.

This happened in just over 12 months, and I will be forever grateful to have met this beautiful soul and help her find her zest for life again!

Since this time, she has not only realised her passion in becoming a coach and helping people change their own lives and rewrite their stories, but she has jumped out of a plane at 15,000 feet AND walked across fire without a single burn.

Talk about self belief and assurance!

Erin has retrained her mind.

She is STRONG, and she no longer feels defined by her past, or blames herself for it either.

Erin used to walk with her head hung, shy and quiet. Yet now she struts, oozing confidence, and leaving a smile on everyone's face wherever she goes.

If she had continued to live believing that she would never be any more than what life had already served her, she may have never found her true calling and been open to following her heart.

The transformation that CAN happen within us all is breathtaking to watch.

We just have to have the guts to get honest about where we are, and if we are happy to continue down the same path.

It's time to smash through our internal glass ceilings and find what we are truly capable of.

YOU'RE ALLOWED TO DRINK FROM THE SPRING FIRST; YOU'RE A LION FOR CHRIST'S SAKE!

Do you carry around a certain level of guilt associated with putting yourself first, or even making yourself some type of priority in the first place?

A lot of us feel that by saying "No" to someone else, but "Yes" to ourselves is selfish and will cause judgement from those around us. We feel that if we put ourselves first, the people we love will suffer because they will be given a smaller portion of our time.

What if I told you that by giving back to yourself, you can then give more freely to others?

Don't you remember what the air hostess tells you every time you hop on a plane?

"Put your own oxygen mask on before fitting one on another".

You're no good to anyone else if you don't take care of you first, and the same goes for how we look after ourselves in any aspect of our life.

For Sarah, she spent years sitting on the sidelines of her children's lives while involved in an abusive relationship. She lived in fear and walked on eggshells, and when the chance came for her to leave the relationship, she could see and feel the positive outcomes of her circumstance. She could play with her kids, and she could look after her, too.

Whilst sadly losing her ex-partner, and the father of her children to suicide, Sarah knew that she had to look after herself now, or the anger, sadness and hatred she felt would be projected and modelled by her children. She could see that if she didn't make herself a priority, and find a way to forgive, then she couldn't help anyone else around her.

Six years on, Sarah understands that looking after herself as a high priority isn't selfish. She has found strength, she has taken her power back, and she has made enormous positive changes to her own life (and that of her children).

Whilst still undertaking a transformation program with me, Sarah has scheduled her kids' extracurricular activities around her own training and coaching. While her kids do their activities, she completes her training and exercise sessions at our studio, picking them up after she's finished. Yes, the juggle of single-parenting is hard, but she has made it work. Her transformation has become a non-negotiable, and she fits the rest of her life around it.

And even better?

Her kids can feel and see the difference in her too, and they are proud of their mum and the person she is as a result of her making herself a priority!

I believe helping ourselves first is selfLESS!

There is absolutely nothing wrong with choosing to work on yourself and anyone who tries to tell you otherwise, or make you feel guilty for it, should know better.

With society carries an expectation that us women should be at the beck and call of our families and have everything together and organised, all of the time.

That is not reality!

When you continue to put yourself at the bottom of your own

priority list, you will breed anger and resentment towards those you love, purely because you aren't feeling the same amount of love that you are giving in return. If you can MAKE (not find) time to love you too, your whole family unit will benefit because you will be happier, healthier and have more energy.

I take my hat off to all the working mums I know who are high achievers, get their kids to all their extra curriculas, have dinner on the table, still make it in to see me for coaching sessions, and love making improvements to themselves physically and mentally each week!

I mean, WOW!

I'm busy enough just with a partner and two fur babies, so I have a great level of respect to the mammas out there!

However, taking the step to look after you first can be daunting and scary. We can begin to feel the resistance and judgement from those around us, and feel like perhaps it isn't our time to work on ourselves and chase our own dreams.

Well, I am here to tell you, there is never a more perfect time than NOW!

Life is short, life is unpredictable, and it can change in a second.

So, if there's been something you've been wanting to do, and you have a passion you wish to pursue, start now without delay, and say "Yes" first, then worry about the finer details later.

When we love what we do, and when we feel happy and fulfilled, we have a light which shines within us, and others can feel it too!

By you stepping up, and working on what you love, you will

in turn help and inspire others to do the same. Tell me, where is the guilt in that?

Sure, if this means your partner has to cook dinner so you can do a few night time hours on your business model, or go to the gym, or read to expand your mind, just make it happen.

My best advice is to ensure you have a support network around you who are going to make sure you take time for you, too.

It's an automatic response to say "Yes" to someone else, even if it interferes with your own plans, so this will require a level of consciousness to stop and think before potentially shooting yourself in the foot.

Start by setting out your non-negotiable YOU time into your calendar or diary.

Think of these as appointments to yourself. You wouldn't cancel last minute on your hair appointment, would you? So, why do we do it to ourselves?

Make sure the times you set are practical and fit around your usual routines and working hours, so as to not place unnecessary pressure on yourself, or make it easy to fob yourself off.

Enlist the help of someone in your inner circle who you know will keep you accountable, and will question you on whether you've done what you need to do or not.

Set some notes around the house to remind you that you are important, and cannot help others to your highest capacity unless you help yourself, too.

Most important of all, ensure your "why" and purpose is clear.

Make time for you because NOT taking steps toward living your purpose could be the most heartbreaking thing of all!

Just remember, life is unpredictable. Do the work now, even when its inconvenient, so future you, and your family can be proud of the leader and inspirer you are!

BECOME YOUR OWN RAVING FAN

There's too many haters and critics in the world already, so why should we be yet another one for ourselves, too?

I mean honestly, if we aren't willing to clap for ourselves, who else is going to?

Becoming proud of yourself for all that you are (and are going to) achieve is the next step for you to unleash your authentic self!

We MUST learn to love and respect ourselves before someone else will.

Searching externally for this sense of significance and respect from another only ends in misery.

'Cause you've heard it before, right? Happiness is an inside job!

In order for us to become our own biggest cheer squad, we must first let our guard down, and let go of the fear that we will be ridiculed. Ever noticed that the ones who try to drag you down are the ones who don't have the guts to do what you do?

I used to be so worried about what my success would breed in others, that I shied away from it. I couldn't take compliments, I downplayed my achievements, and I certainly didn't stop to smell the roses either!

When I took note of the type of people who were critiquing me, I saw this pattern emerge. What I finally saw was that their words had absolutely nothing to do with me, and everything to do with them. It wasn't a reflection of me at all; I had only allowed myself to feel defined and weighed down by the negativity.

By becoming my own fan, I could swipe away self doubt and fear of rejection because I knew at the end of the day, that it only mattered that I was happy with who I was and what I was working on. The opinions of others which I so desperately craved only dragged me down because I did not yet believe in myself, so I continued to look outwardly for this belief instead.

I had to learn to clap for myself and become my own fan!

It's not an easy feat to take compliments from others, let alone ourselves, but this alone is what directly impacted how I felt about myself and the work I was doing.

When I started the habit of highlighting my achievements, instead of downplaying them, it didn't matter what someone else thought of me anymore; it only mattered what I thought.

I knew that if I continued to look outwardly for feedback, for accolades and for acceptance, I would soon be heading down a long, slippery road. Other people's opinions are subjective, and not at all a reflection on myself in the first place anyway!

Earlier last year in fact, I nominated myself for a local business award. I already knew what I did was awesome (yes, when you're your own fan you can talk about yourself in this way!), but I still hung on to that need for validation to make sure I was on the right track.

I worked long and hard on my nomination entry, and felt pretty bloody chuffed reading it back to myself. However, when it finally came time to announce the finalists, I was upset to see that I hadn't been selected. Okay, okay, I was more than upset, I was gutted!

I had worked tirelessly on not just my entry, but for the last three years, so to see that other businesses had been announced as finalists over me was hard.

Yes, the road to developing higher levels of consciousness and personal growth is long, and full of lessons! Sometimes when I think I've got it all together, another lesson hits me and I see how long I still have to go!

This was one of those lessons.

I was searching for validation STILL from people who didn't know me, and didn't directly matter, yet was upset that they didn't give me the pat on the back I had hoped for.

Instead, the validation I should have been focusing on was right in front of me: they were my family of members who are the reason why I do what I do each day.

When I remembered this, I could look around at them and what they were achieving, and be proud both for them, and for myself for helping them along the way.

And this was so much more important than any $10 trophy based on the opinion of a stranger!

Now, it's time for you to become your own fan, too!

When you're about to do a task, complete a presentation, or compete in your chosen sport, do you give yourself a pep up and a high 5? Or do you meekly wish for yourself that you'll do okay, and "not fail"?

If the inner lion in you is weak and quiet over these times, the level of commitment you throw into the task will be lessened to the amount you could give.

But, when you are a FAN of what you do, and you believe in what you do, you will give so much heart into the task that you are captivating, you are confident and you are successful!

How do we go from meek and quiet to releasing an almighty roar?

Practise!

List all that you have achieved.
Saying it in your head simply isn't enough as our minds have a way of distorting things. Instead, you need to write down all that you have accomplished which you are proud of, and how these accomplishments have helped you get to where you are now, and where you plan on going.

Then, start to shift your awareness to whose approval, accolades and praise you crave most.
Write down these names, and ask yourself WHY you crave their approval?
What is it about them that makes you feel the need for their acceptance and pats on the back?
Are these people positive influences in your life, or negative? And do they directly affect what you do anyway?

When you can begin to identify why you crave external validation, you can start to rewire your mind to first find validation in yourself, before others.
Validation without an agenda, without fear of rejection, and

instead, just validation with love and kindness.

And this has to start from within.

Am I a good person?

What am I proud of?

Have I done a good job?

Where could I make some improvements to better myself?

Your internal love and acceptance breeds a higher level of love and acceptance from those closest to you: the positive people in your life who help make you better, and not those whose acceptance you crave simply because you don't get enough of it!

When you clap for yourself, you'll empower a cheer squad of loyal friends and family around you, who clap for you when you deserve it (which is always, by the way), but who also help you see when you need to shift your focus to allow for more growth and development.

These people only appear for us when we can believe it in ourselves first.

We can all sense someone's lack of self belief from a mile away, and when we are around them, we feel uncertain because we can FEEL the lack of trust they have in their own abilities. This is why it's so important to find those reasons "why" you are worthy, you are good enough, and why you should back yourself.

Another method to assist us in becoming our own fan is to celebrate every win, no matter how small!

You nailed your presentation at work? WIN!

You finished a task you've been putting off? WIN!

You consciously took charge of a poor habit and adopted a new
routine? WIN!

No matter how big or small, celebration is essential!

And no, I don't mean taking yourself out for cake each time (although, sometimes this is very acceptable).

Instead, find a new routine that you complete every time you have a win.

This could be giving yourself a high-5, putting on your favourite song, or yelling out a big "YES"!

In our studio, we have a Tibetan gong.

Every time someones makes an achievement or beats a personal best, they ring the gong, and the rest of us cheer.

Now, whenever I hear that gong, I can't help but feel amazing and happy because the sound brings such a positive meaning!

ACTION TASK!

What words does my inner critic speak to me most often, and when?

Who do I compare yourself to and why? What do they really have that I don't think I do?

How can I make time for myself and the things which bring me joy?

What is something that happened in my past, which has caused me to think I'm not capable of achieving my version of success?

Whose validation do I crave the most, and why?
Are they positive or negative influences to my life?
What will their validation ACTUALLY give me? Would it really make me feel any different toward myself if I received it?

What am I most proud of?
When I think back to this time, did I have TRUST and BELIEF in my own abilities?

Take action NOW!

How can you now begin to put the wheels of change in motion?

What can you do with your new-found knowledge to allow your inner lion to shine, so you push yourself head-first into action?

Well, before getting into things, I want to tell you a story about someone no longer with us, but always in my thoughts.

Loren was 27, and had her whole life ahead of her but unfortunately the universe had other plans when we lost her tragically and suddenly in her sleep, for reasons still unknown.

Loren lived her life saying "Yes" to opportunity. She had fears, doubts and insecurities, like we all do, but she was one to follow her gut, and do what felt "right" to her.

Something Loren and her partner were extremely passionate about was travelling. It would have been easy to follow the status quo at their age and buy a house and settle down, but to them, seeing the world was more important and fulfilling at the time.

The year of her passing, Loren quit her job as a teacher to spend three months travelling with friends, and one month following with her partner.

She was scared to travel alone for so long, and she received backlash from people who didn't understand how her partner could trust her going off on her own adventure. But trust is built on trust, and they firmly believed this.

A pinnacle moment which forced a hand in her decision to say "Yes" was the realisation that her current job was not giving her the growth she needed. Their values and beliefs no longer aligned, and she didn't feel she could help change the lives of her students to the capacity she wanted to.

So, she made the decision to relief teach before and after her travels so she could find a school that was the right fit for her and where she wanted to go.

Sadly, she never did get the chance to find the perfect school for her, however she had big dreams.

In her future, Loren had plans to be an author.

From her words, you can see she believed in paving her own path, regardless of the opinions of others: "You are meant to follow your path of happiness. You are meant to keep moving, and that will mean moving on. Others do not understand, but they will if you show them, rather than trying to justify your bold ideas. Show them. Show yourself. You can do this."

She was talented, spiritual, believed in the power of the universe, and she questioned the meaning of her life and her thoughts. Her passion was trees. She loved to take photos of trees of any shape or size, and I guess in some way, to her they signified growth, prosperity and the cycle of life.

Life can change in an instant, so we should all stop worrying about what could go wrong, and start dreaming about what could go RIGHT instead!

It brings me comfort in my thoughts for Loren, because I

know she followed her heart, and she chased adventure in those months prior to her death. She didn't shy away from her fears, instead she pushed herself into some amazing experiences.

I hope that hearing this has made you realise that, while life is short, and death is cruel, we can all have the desire to go head-first into pursuing what we want.

Fear is inevitable, but mediocrity doesn't have to be.

We are all so scared of what could go wrong, of taking a risk, of going on adventures, of doing something that scares us.

But what if we knew that tomorrow wasn't guaranteed?

Would we jump out of a plane, would we learn to scuba dive, would we book that one way plane ticket?

Because if we wonder about the potential risks in these activities, we should also think about the potential risks in every day life too: driving to work, riding our bikes, or going to sleep at night.

If there's one thing I have learnt, it's that we aren't here forever, and in order to accept that perhaps we should worry less about the "what if's", and focus more on the legacy we wish to leave behind.

So now, let's put thought into action so you can create a masterpiece of your life, and find true happiness within your inner lion.

LIONS SPEAK WITH INTEGRITY

Are you the type to follow through when you say you'll do something?

For me, my word is my bond, and integrity is one of the strongest core values I hold.

Gonna, wanna, coulda and shoulda are all just words without significance and without intent unless they are followed by action!

If you truly want to change your life, achieve your dreams and become the kick ass woman you know you are, then it's time to put meaning into the words you speak.

Actions speak louder than words, and too many times I have heard the phrase "I was gonna, but… (insert excuse here)".

Put intention and action into your words. If you want to do something, this is your time to do it. No more playing small, no more excuses, no more "shoulda's" or "buts".

You don't have to have the answers to start, you just need a clear vision of where you want to go, and most importantly, why you want to do it, before putting some goals in place, rolling up your sleeves and getting to work.

Yes, it's easier said than done, and that's precisely why a large majority of people don't speak with intent or integrity.

Because the work is hard, it's often uncomfortable, and it comes with sacrifice.

I can assure you that the road less travelled can bring about a life you only used to dream about.

Lions don't say they're gonna hunt, but instead spend the afternoon napping in the dry grass.

No, they damn well hunt, because they are all too aware of the implications of NOT following their word. They are leaders and have families to feed, just like you and I do.

Integrity is such a strong value of mine that I use it to hold myself accountable for the words I speak. If I tell someone I'm going to do something, I'll do it, and I'll use it as a personal form of blackmail to further help me continue in the action phase (for I know if I don't, I'm no longer just letting myself down, but someone else too)!

By now I hope you are at the stage where you know what you want, and the direction you need to take, and are ready to conquer it.

And if you aren't quite there yet?

That's okay, I can guarantee you are probably a hell of a lot closer to gaining some answers than you were when you first picked up this book.

What level of accountability are you ready to place on the words you speak?

Are you ready to finally follow through and make yourself proud for taking some form of action (no matter how big or small)?

DEALING WITH THE INNER PERFECTIONIST

What is your relationship with perfection?

Do you hold yourself back because you believe if you don't get it "right" or "perfect" on the first go, then there's no use trying in the first place?

Well, it's time to begin to manage the expectations you place on yourself.
Are they justifiable?
Or would others say that they're ridiculous?

This has been something I have had to work on myself over the years. I grew up as a perfectionist with high standards both on myself and others. I used to worry that I wouldn't get things right first go, or that I'd make a mistake and have to spend time fixing it.
I've come to remind myself (often) that I am human; mistakes are inevitable, but they also serve as learning tools.
Yes, sometimes shit does hit the fan and I have to spend a significant amount of time re-doing my work or fixing a situation. However, I always made sure I learnt from my mistakes.

We tend to have a habit of waiting for the PERFECT time to start something new, to make a change in our lives, or to do a particular activity or task.
People spend so much time procrastinating and preparing, that they never actually leave the start line. Or, when they do, they've often left themselves with little time to finish!
This can lead to us adopting unhealthy routines or methods

in which to finish the task. Something I hear way too often as a trainer is "I just need to lose five kilos THEN I'll start exercising".

Don't laugh, I know you've either heard this or used it as an excuse yourself at some point.

I often wonder when someone does tell me this, if they realise how ridiculous it sounds as it leaves their own mouth, too?

When we fear not perfecting things first go, we use shitty excuses and reasoning to buy ourselves time so that when we are finally "ready" to start, we can succeed right off the bat.

But life is unpredictable, and curve balls will be sent hurtling our way often.

The inner perfectionist will use these so called "curveballs" as an excuse not to do something, or to hold themselves back from opportunity because the timing isn't right.

But, the inner realist will adapt and conquer regardless of the circumstance.

It's about having a healthy balance!

Whilst I do believe self-expectation is a good thing, it shouldn't be at the expense of you trying to be so perfect that you never leave the start line.

It's about deciding what level of expectation you demand from yourself, whilst still being able to adapt and change your plans if need be. There are countless methods we can use to get a task done, and sometimes we may not do them how we "like" to, but if we can do them in a way which is necessary for getting the job done, then cut yourself some slack and do it!

At the end of the day, I guess you need to ask yourself "What's more important to me? Getting the job done, or doing it absolutely perfectly?"

I would say completion rules perfection.

Sure, set yourself a bar of execution you'd like to achieve, but if you fall just short of it, that's okay. I mean, you could always go back and make some adjustments if you need to at a later date, or don't. It's entirely up to you.

For me personally, some days I struggle to get to the gym to do my own training. If I feel bogged down in work, or tired and lethargic, I often ask myself "Is it more important for me to rest or to train today? Which will help future Zoe the most?"

If training is my answer, then sure, I may not work to the capacity I usually do, but the fact that I'm there is what counts most. I used to struggle with this because I would want to smash out a killer session, every session. But sometimes my body just can't do that and this is something I've had to accept, so instead I will adapt what I'm doing to suit how I feel.

I still get a sense of accomplishment in completing my training, however I don't allow room to beat myself up for doing a poor job.

That's what I call a win-win!

I learnt quickly that perfection was boring.

It's like colouring within the lines ALL the time without having the freedom to explore the other side of the line.

Sounds pretty miserable, right?

Never really changing, learning or growing for fear of moving to the outside of the lines where the uncontrollables and unknown lives.

A lot of our perfectionist tendencies comes from the feeling of needing to be in control and have it all together, all of the time.

But if you can change your relationship with the uncontrollables, and use them as a positive, instead of a negative, your level of happiness will dramatically change for the better.

Because why do we let things which we cannot control throw us off so often?

Like the weather. Or the traffic.

We can't control them, so why allow them to ruin our plans when we can instead adapt and simply worry about what we can focus on and change?

If you continue to let these uncontrollable factors run your day, and ruin your mood, then how are you treating those around you? And what type of energy are you putting out into the world?

The perfectionist tries to control all uncontrollables and outcomes, but we simply can't.

The sooner we can let go of this and accept it, the better. Allowing external influences to shape our mood won't make us happy, or allow us to feel fulfilled long term. Instead, we need to take responsibility for what we can control, and accept those in which we can't.

It's the only way.

This is something I have had to learn over the years, too. We can't control what anyone else thinks, feels, says, or does; but we can only control how we react to what they do.

We can't try to control another person so that they speak or behave in harmony with us, because we are all different and unique, and must accept each other's opinions, values and choices as theirs, and theirs alone.

If you feel as if you are constantly chasing your tail and taking one step forward but two steps back, let's evaluate your current level of "perfectionism":

- Do you start things, but often don't finish if the work you've done isn't quite up to scratch?
- Do you say "No" when someone offers help, because you believe you can do it better yourself (regardless of exhaustion or burn out)?
- Do you put off starting things while you wait for the timing to be right?
- Do you criticise your own work, even if it's great?
- Do you become angry or frustrated easily when someone or something affects your original plans?

Well then, if you answered "Yes" to any of these questions, you exhibit some of the traits of a perfectionist!

As I have said above, it's about learning to control your controllables, whilst managing the expectations you place on yourself.

Sooner or later you are going to realise that you cannot continue to meet your own ridiculous standards, and instead you'll have to make compromises in order to move forward and get shit done!

I'm not saying you do things poorly; I'm just saying that it's time to cut yourself some slack.

Because sometimes getting the job done, and putting ticks in the boxes as you work toward your goals is more important than getting it done right or perfectly first go anyway.

Life will always require you to adapt and change in order to meet the needs of each individual situation. So, better to start learning to adapt now than continue living between those tiny, perfect lines you currently do!

OUT WITH THE OLD, IN WITH THE NEW ... RULES, THAT IS!

Are there rules you have given yourself over your life that you continue to attach to, regardless of whether they still hold true for you?

Do you continue to follow old rules or rituals, even if they no longer make sense to you?

As humans, we like having rules to follow, and we like to set boundaries for ourselves based on what we "should" and "shouldn't" do.

We often create these rules when we are in a different stage of our lives, but forget to adjust them when things change. These rules that we live with define what we do and how we respond or react to events or circumstances throughout our day.

No wonder we feel so God damn annoyed and frustrated at ourselves when we can't follow our own unnecessary rules system each day!

When we feel bound by our own rules or rituals which no longer serve us, we feel trapped with no space to move or grow. They hold us back from saying "Yes" to opportunities, and they stop us from creating space for new, more effective rules. We fill our plate with these old rules so much, that there becomes no room for us to create new ones.

The thing is, the rules we give ourselves don't have to define us, our character, or who we are. Unless we let them.

If you're finding that you are following in-ground rituals or rules that are holding you back, perhaps it's time to re-evaluate them!

A rule I have chosen to remove recently is: "I don't do upside-down rides".

Along with my fear of rollercoasters, I had a fear of being upside down, or suspended mid-air. But, I always saw these rides and a small part of me always wanted to go for a spin anyway, yet I was held back because my own rule was that I couldn't.

You see, these rules always make perfect sense at the time of creation, but when we assess them later, we realise that they are completely unnecessary.

Since realising that this old rule was bullshit, and was holding me back from a lot of fun in my life, I have consciously chosen to break my own rule and have a go when I see a ride I want to try.

Not only this, but each time I have broken my old rule, I have created space to create a new rule for myself, one which will help me have fun and push myself.

Now, instead of the old rule of "I don't do upside down rides", my new rule is "I'll give it a crack, if the idea of it both scares and excites me".

This new rule gives me the space I need to push out of my comfort zone, and to learn that I can do anything I put my mind to, if I want to. And since doing so, I'm starting to thrive off trying new experiences, and I can feel excited when I envision myself accomplishing something that I used to say "No" to.

A common rule for a lot of people could be: "I won't go to an event, party or seminar on my own".

Understand the reason you created this rule in the first place was probably to remove fear and discomfort, but know that you could miss out on a lot of great opportunities if you continue to refuse to fly solo. If you really want to grow and succeed, understand that this old rule is causing you to avoid the things you need in your life.

If we want to become the person we have been dreaming of, at some point, we have to learn to walk alone; this is inevitable. So, create a new rule which supports you going to great events and workshops alone, because who knows, you may meet some incredible people you wouldn't have if you'd gone with someone else.

It's time to ask yourself:

- What rules are you living by which you know are holding you back?
- How are these old rules stopping you from getting to where you want to go, or from having fun?
- What is a new rule you can replace it with to allow you to stretch yourself?
- What is the likely outcome of following this new rule instead?

I know for myself, that when I could let go of those ridiculous rules that "old Zoe" had created, I made space for a lot more fun and excitement in my life.

LEARNING TO CHANGE YOUR STATE

To me, "state" is simply the mood or energy which we feel, and put out to the world. Having the ability to change your emotions, and how you feel in a split second is going to be a worthwhile tool for you moving forward.

I've spoken throughout the book about how easy it is to become trapped in our thoughts as they spiral out of control, but it doesn't have to be this way. You can give yourself your power back by changing how you feel in an instant, to better utilise your time for happiness and productivity over doubt and worry.

Remember my story in the fears chapter about how I assumed the wonder woman pose prior to hopping on that rollercoaster? Or how I chanted "cool moss" before walking across fire?

These were methods adopted to change my "state" and how I feel.

By having the ability to change my state, I can influence my results for the better. I can increase my confidence and self-belief, I can do something that scares me (and survive!), and I can control the way in which I respond to potential problems or situations.

Emotions drive what we do.

If we can change our current state to allow for an increase in performance, and a higher level of focus, wouldn't you do it?

Not only this, but if we can put ourselves in an optimum state at a moments notice, we can emit a level of energy from within us that makes other people WANT to be around us!

I'm sure you probably know someone who is constantly wound up, stressed and anxious, and being around them makes you feel uptight and skittish just by being in their presence. On the other side of this, you'll probably have someone in your life who emits a level of energy in which you can't explain, yet you love to be around them. Being in their company makes you feel lighter, happier, and more engaged to the world around you; it's like being on a natural high.

Well, you can do the same when you learn how to change your state for the better.

You don't have to wait until you achieve something to feel great; you can start right now.
You can have the tools to harness your peak state, too.
You can learn to anticipate, but NOT react, to your habits or thoughts which breed suffering or worry.

Gaining the ability to change your state is easy, once you know how. However, it requires you to stay conscious in your thoughts and your emotions.
We know that we all think in harmony with our subconscious mind, but if we continue to react the same, think the same, and use the same, negative language, we will find more resistance in changing to become the person we are desperate to be!

It's easy to stay in your emotional comfort zone because in there we feel certainty. But like with all comfort zones, it's not pushing us to reach higher potentials.
You have to become aware of your patterns in order to break them!

What triggers stress, worry or overwhelm within you?
What thoughts do you give negative meaning to?
What makes you feel as if you are not enough?

It's such an ingrained habit to have negative responses to what is happening to us, that we forget to think about what is happening FOR us.

We allow ourselves to continue to feel unhappy and unfulfilled by staying in the same state, instead of demanding more from ourselves.

It also needs to become HABIT to change your state for the better, in a moment's notice.

We can do this via a number of methods, however all must be done whilst in conscious thought.

Movement is one of the quickest and easiest ways to change our state instantly.

When we feel sad, angry, or despair, what are we most likely doing? Sitting and stewing on these thoughts, so much so that they begin a vicious cycle.

When you feel these feelings come on, and can anticipate what's coming by being aware of your own triggers, get up and MOVE!

Any movement is positive movement, but do it with purpose.

Dance, run, star jump, kick, punch. Move your whole body as quickly as you can and I can almost guarantee that as soon as you do, you will feel completely different once you sit down again.

Another way to change your state is to actively laugh and

joke about the negative thoughts you are having. Don't fight them off, instead let them float by, laughing at their absurdity while they pass by. Something I do often is I pretend my worries and thoughts are attached by a cord from the top of my head. I visualise them swaying to and fro, before taking a pair of scissors, cutting the cord, and waving as I watching them drift away.

Gratitude is another incredibly powerful feeling which can dull negativity instantly. When things start spiralling out of control, hold onto a feeling or a memory that brings you happiness and gratitude. Find something that can become a safe haven for you in times of need and remember how you felt, what you smelt, and what you saw when you think back to this memory.

For some, having a photograph of this happy memory is helpful, as it can be hard to reach for gratitude without something tangible to hold onto, so place a photo somewhere you can find easily, and look at often.

You could also do what I have done and adopt the wonder woman pose.

By breaking the pattern and disrupting your thoughts and emotions, you have consciously chosen NOT to allow them to take power over you.

And that in itself is empowering!

You can change your state at any time you need; just understand that doing so in itself can become a new, positive ritual for you. Whenever you feel your mood begin to shift, go straight for your peak state and stay there!

The more practice you get at this, the easier it will become. I know for myself, I didn't realise how much suffering I was causing myself, and how much negativity I was emitting into the world, until I learnt that I could change my state at the click of my fingers.

I was the only one who could do that for myself, and when I did, everything in my life became easier and better. I found a level of energy I didn't know was within me, my outlook became brighter, and things that used to worry me on end became something I could easily brush off.

Now, I'm not saying that learning to change your state is a cure-all. It isn't.

But, it is a tool you can adopt right now to help give you positive momentum to work toward what it is you truly want!

WHAT IS YOUR VERSION OF HAPPINESS? IT'S TIME TO LIVE IT!

Well, now that you've made your way this far into the book (well done by the way!), it's time to begin to create your own version of happiness and fulfilment.

Ask yourself now, what is it that you truly want?

Despite fear, despite impracticalities, and despite any excuse or barriers which try to form in your mind, simply be honest with yourself. There is no time like the present!

What do you want to do?

What type of person do you want to be, and how do you want others to feel when they are in your aura?

What has your inner lion been trying to tell you all these years, that up until now, you have been pushing away?

Yes, I know she's in there, and by now she's bursting to come out!

It's time to stop ignoring that little niggle inside your gut and finally listen and accept what it is that you desire.

Understand that your true happiness will lie in following this inner voice.

The more you resist it, the more you pretend it isn't there, and the more you let those bullshit excuses get in your way, the bigger the hole of unfulfilment.

We spend so many days, months and years of our lives trying to find happiness and fulfilment from external things, whilst completing ignoring the one source of it all: ourselves!

It's time to stop and listen.

It's time to change your perceptions, your habits and your thinking styles which continue to hold you back, and instead look within and answer that muffled roar you've been burying away.

I hope that by now, you are feeling clearer on your goals, your purpose, and what it is that is driving you to live the version of success you crave!

Know that you are capable of achieving it, you just have to trust yourself and allow your inner lion and intuition to guide you down your new path.

Yes, there will be lessons, mistakes and stumbles along the way, but these all open the door for opportunity and growth at a later date. Don't avoid them, don't be paralysed by fear; just keep placing one foot in front of the other, allowing your lion to steer you to greatness!

> The time for real, raw, no holds barred honesty is now.
> What exactly is it that you want in your life?

Take a moment to think about the perfect day for you.
What are you doing?
Who are you with?
How do you feel?

Soak this feeling in.

And if you feel drawn back by the "What ifs?", take a few deep breaths, push those thoughts away, and continue to picture your ideal day, for this forms the version of your life you want to live.

Imagine you are an artist with a blank canvas; you have the opportunity to create anything you want, so what are you going to do?

You sure as shit aren't going to start painting the workplace you hate, sadness, loneliness, or a lack of wealth, will you?

So, what will you create for yourself, instead?

ACTION TASK!

Will future me thank me for saying "Yes" to someone else, but "No" to myself?
How can I set up accountability systems which work for me?
What have I been "gonna" do for years, but haven't?

What have my perfectionist tendencies been stopping me from achieving or starting?
What is the worst possible outcome if I don't complete a task perfectly? How detrimental would this actually be to my life?
How can I learn to let go of the unrealistic expectations I place on myself?

Do I want to feel chained to my emotions each day, or do I want control over them?
What rituals can I adopt to help me change my own state?

What rules am I ready to re-write for myself, and which current rules no longer serve me?

Record my version of an "ideal day" in as much detail as possible. What do I see, hear, smell and taste? Is this vision bright, or dark? Happy, or sad? Does it feel close up in my mind, or far away?
You may find this vision is a lot different now for you, than when it was when you started this book.
Now that you have explored this again, how can you begin to change your current existence, and start working toward living out your "ideal day"?

Go forth and ROAR!

An important thing to keep in mind is successful people don't live their lives by luck and chance. They don't wait for life to happen to them; they create it!

They open up opportunities, feed their desires and dreams, they build their own paths, and they most definitely don't apologise to others for working on themselves!

If someone tries to tell you that "you're just lucky", remember that it's simply a term lazy people use to describe another's success. They refuse to acknowledge the blood, sweat, tears and determination that you have invested into yourself, merely because they are afraid to do the same.

YOU have the power in your hands and you are resilient enough to work hard for what you believe in.

Your inner lion creates her own life, because she has the confidence to do so. No, not in the absence of fear, but in the presence of it. Your inner lion feels the fear and does it anyway, for fear does not crumble her; instead, it strengthens her.

Just remember, success is a journey.

It sure as hell doesn't happen overnight. It takes months and years of perseverance and hard work. It's about making mistakes and learning from them. It's feeling like you need to take one step back, to take one step forward again. It's working on habits which have held you back for years. It's accepting responsibility for your actions, and realising that a new approach is required.

It's saying "No" to that voice in your head which is telling you that you aren't good enough.

And it's a whole lot of sweat, tears, choice words, joy, pride and support.

If the process were easy, we'd all have what we really want, right?

Probably.

The question worth asking is, would you appreciate it if it came easy?

Would you look back on the journey proud of how much you'd grown and how far you'd come?

'Cause that's where the magic is!

It's the smile on your face when you say "YES" to you, to allow room for growth and prosperity in your life. It's that second of pause and stillness while you prepare for your next move.

And it's the way you can finally admit that after all these years, you love yourself and who you have become.

My question to you as we wrap things up here is this:

Are you willing to do what (your version of) success demands, in order to create a life where you live by the ruling of your own inner lion?

Or, will you remain slave to your own insecurities, negative perceptions and uninspiring beliefs that are stopping you from becoming who you truly are?

The choice is yours, and yours alone.

However, I urge you to unlock that cage and let yourself roar, for you will demand a quality of life for yourself that others can only dream about.

And you will never, ever be the same again.

UNCAGE THE LION WITHIN

Acknowledgements

This book would not have been possible without the help from a few incredible people in my life.

To Trish - If it weren't for you, I doubt I would have ever started this book. The car rides up to Melbourne all those weekends helped pave the way for me to begin my writing journey. You support me, you stand by me, and you keep me accountable. You help me find the confidence in myself when I can't find it for myself. I feel extremely grateful to have you in my life, and to have found a second family in you, so thank you.

To Jase - Your unwavering support and honest truths help me when I need it the most. It is because of you I can throw myself head first into the tasks and projects which bring my life meaning and happiness, knowing that if anything were to happen, you would be there to hold my hand while I put myself back together again. I love you, always.

To Jeanette and Jeff (the Boss Parents) - Thankyou for supporting me to become the best version of me I can be. I'm bloody proud to call you my Mum and Dad, and of the upbringing you provided me with. Even though the extent of my dreams and ambitions may not always be clear, you support me and help me on my path regardless. Thank you for being the raving, loving fans I needed you to be.

To Erin (Lil Boss) - What a wild ride it's already been! I am so grateful to have you by my side on this big adventure. Thank you for coming into my life, for finding the confidence to trust and love yourself, and for opening up to a world of possibility, even when you could only see the first couple of steps. Big things are coming, and I am so lucky to have you as a constant support and partner in crime.

To Sarah - Your undying loyalty has shown me the value of having the right people in my pride. And you are one of those right people for me! I am so proud of your tenacity, inner strength, and love that you show despite any shortcomings or hard times in your life. Thank you for your constant love and support. Please never change, we all love you as you are, despite your ability to talk underwater!

To my amazing "ZHT family" - Thankyou all so much for being on this journey with me. Thank you for putting your trust and faith in me, for allowing me to help you build the path for your own journey, and for the love and support you show everyone at ZHT. Without you all, we wouldn't be the community we are today. You have all helped in making my dreams a reality, so thank you for holding faith in my journey, and trusting in what we can do for you, too.

If you'd like to get in touch, please don't hesitate to do so.
www.zoehyde.com.au
zoe@zoehyde.com.au
Follow me on Instagram @ zoehyde.author
Join our online Facebook Group "Uncage The Lion Within"
to continue to feed your mind and follow the calling of your
own inner lion.

UNCAGE THE LION WITHIN

www.ingramcontent.com/pod-product-compliance
Lightning Source LLC
Chambersburg PA
CBHW031415290426
44110CB00011B/386